Business Finance

Business Finance

A pictorial guide for managers

Paul Burns and Peter Morris

BUTTERWORTH
HEINEMANN

Butterworth-Heinemann
Linacre House, Jordan Hill, Oxford OX2 8DP
A division of Reed Educational and Professional Publishing Ltd

 A member of the Reed Elsevier plc group

OXFORD BOSTON JOHANNESBURG
MELBOURNE NEW DELHI SINGAPORE

First published 1994
Reprinted 1997

British Library Cataloguing in Publication Data
A catalogue record for this book is available from the British Library

ISBN 0 7506 1899 X

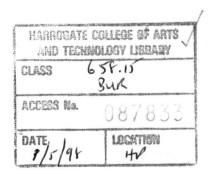
Printed and bound at The Bath Press, Bath.

Foreword

Whatever the shape or size of a business, they all have one thing in common - they hope to make money. In this respect at least, there are only two kinds: successful and unsuccessful. A major factor in determining success is the ability of management to control its finances.

This book painlessly demystifies the process of accounting and the understanding of business finance. It shows you what information needs to be produced, how to go about producing it, and then how to interpret and use it. We have invented a small company in the furniture-making trade and traced its progress over the first couple of years of its life. The business is started by two people with considerable expertise in making furniture but none in making - or handling - business finance. They are heading for disaster, going through the "Death Valley Curve", until a friendly financial expert takes a hand... but read the rest for yourself.

The book will, we feel sure, be of interest not only to those who have responsibility for their company's finances but to the rest of us, for whom money plays a necessary part of life. Understanding business finance might even prove to be fun!

Paul Burns
Peter Morris

April 1994

Contents

1 How Money Works in Business

Businesses come in all shapes and sizes, but they all have one thing in common. However big or small they are, **money** works in exactly the same way for all of them.

Jack Plank and his partner, Andy Mann, have just started their own business.

They are going to make hand-crafted furniture for a discerning clientele.

It's a very small firm, consisting of Jack, Andy, Vera the secretary and Robin, the apprentice, although Jack plans to employ more craftsmen later. The premises of Fine Furniture comprise a workshop and an office. Their machinery and plant, newly bought, is the usual collection of lathes, benches tools, sundry equipment and a van.

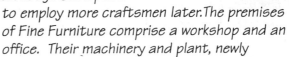

Jack is the senior partner.

He's going to have to keep track of how well the business is doing, while Andy makes sure the furniture is made properly, and on time.

Jack has a problem....

....Although Jack can see whether his business is functioning **efficiently**...

...spot areas where some improvement is possible...

...and get an idea of the firm's performance as a provider of quality products, there's one thing he can't see.

Even if he watches things all day and every day, he can't find out

how much money the company is making.

Of course, from time to time, the bank lets Jack know what the business has in its account, but bank statements raise as many questions as they answer.

For instance, they don't show how much the business owes - or is owed; how much valuable stock they've already bought; how much money should be kept back for wages or the replacement of equipment. One thing is certain...

what's in the bank ISN'T PROFIT

Jack will need to know all these things if he's going to succeed.

He's going to need two kinds of information.

Without accurate financial information he won't be in a position to make financial decisions when he needs to.

1 **How much money the company has, and where it is invested**

This kind of information is like a snapshot of the company's finances - the resources it has at a particular moment.

2 **How that money has grown (or shrunk)**

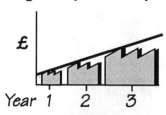

This kind of information is a report on how the business has performed over a particular period.

These two kinds of financial information are usually presented like this:

Balance Sheet

Where the money comes from - and where it is invested

Profit and Loss Statement

How the money has grown (or shrunk) through trading

This information will enable you to take advantage of opportunities for, or minimise threats to, the business in the future.

Now let's take a look at Fine Furniture and ask these two questions:

I foresee great trouble ahead...

Where has the money come from - and where is it invested?

How has the money grown (or shrunk) through trading over a certain period?

Where is the company's money?

When Jack and his partner decided to go into business together they needed a certain amount of capital to get going.

Some of it came from savings.

Some of it came from friends and relatives who thought Jack and Andy would do well in business together, so they were prepared to risk some money on the company.

Some of it came from the bank in the form of a short-term loan.

This is called

SHARE CAPITAL

Jack and Andy well understood the risk they were taking with their savings, but what they needed to know was that there was a lot of difference between loan capital and share capital.

This is called

LOAN CAPITAL

PAYING FOR LOAN CAPITAL

Although the bank will have been satisfied enough about Fine Furniture's future prospects to lend them money in the first place, they'll want interest on the loan to be paid regularly whether the business is profitable or not, They will also want the loan repaid on the due date.

whereas...

PAYING FOR SHARE CAPITAL

..the shareholders of the firm will want to be rewarded through a regular dividend for the risk they are taking by investing in it, but they will have to accept smaller returns on their investment if the business does badly. They could even risk losing their money altogether if the firm goes broke although they would prefer to make a large capital gain on their investment.

So they also share in success, whereas the bank goes on getting the same return on its investment, more or less.

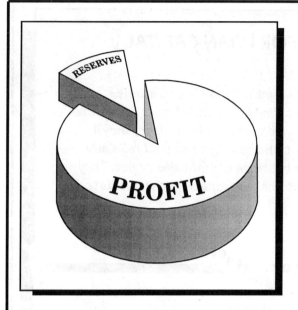

There's a third source of capital, which becomes available after the business has been trading successfully for a while.

Some money can be put aside to help finance the running of the business. It comes out of the profits, and it's called the **reserves.**

Reserves are the profits left in the business after tax and dividends have been paid. They are a major source of finance in profitable companies, but Fine Furniture wouldn't have access to any reserves yet. Remember, they've just started trading, so they don't have any profits.

RECAP ON WHERE A BUSINESS'S MONEY COMES FROM

The money in any business comes from one of three sources.

SHARE CAPITAL

LOAN CAPITAL

RESERVES

But how is this cash to be spent?

Jack and Andy have no shortage of things to spend money on.

They have a long list: business premises, a van, raw materials, plant and equipment; business stationery, wages for themselves and anyone they employ; money for the electricity bills, phones and so on...and on.

So this is where the company's money is spent...

Building
van
raw materials
plant
stationery
wages
computer
phone
furniture
electricity

The items on the company's long shopping list can be divided into three categories...

Things the business needs to go directly into what it sells	**Things the business needs but are not intended for sale**	**Things the business must pay for whether it trades or not**

These costs cover items like raw materials, production-related costs like factory heat, light and power, wages for factory workers.	*These costs cover items that have to be bought to produce the business's goods or services, like vehicles, buildings, tools.*	*These costs cover items like the rent and rates, telephone bills, stationery, office staff salaries and other administration costs.*
Money needed for these is called	*The money tied up in these items is called*	*The money spent on this we call*
WORKING CAPITAL.	**FIXED ASSETS.**	**ADMIN COSTS.**

It's important to make a distinction between money spent and money invested

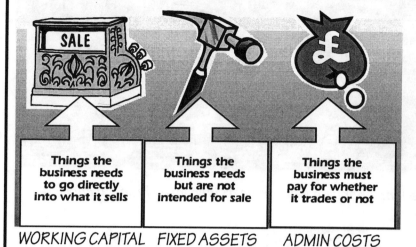

| Things the business needs to go directly into what it sells | Things the business needs but are not intended for sale | Things the business must pay for whether it trades or not |

WORKING CAPITAL   FIXED ASSETS   ADMIN COSTS

Of these three categories, the first two - working capital and fixed assets - represent the money the company invests to make it successful. The third category, its admin costs, represents the money it has to spend just to exist. What it gets spent on will not add to the value of the company.

Because admin costs are an expense, not an investment, they are not shown on the balance sheet. They reduce the profit of the firm; or, if there were no profit, they would reduce the company's reserves. So, if we were to ask "Where does the money come from, and where is it spent?" we would get this:.

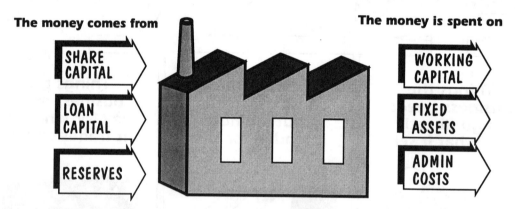

The money comes from

SHARE CAPITAL

LOAN CAPITAL

RESERVES

The money is spent on

WORKING CAPITAL

FIXED ASSETS

ADMIN COSTS

Whereas, if we were to ask our original question (page 3) "Where does the money come from, and where is it invested?" we would get this:

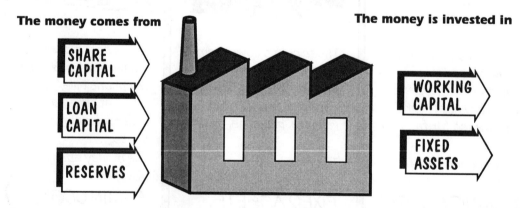

The money comes from

SHARE CAPITAL

LOAN CAPITAL

RESERVES

The money is invested in

WORKING CAPITAL

FIXED ASSETS

This is a truer indicator of the wealth of the company, and is the information you will find in the balance sheet.

There's a
**fundamental difference
between
working capital and fixed assets**

Jack and Andy are going to buy the best FIXED ASSETS they can afford with the money they have available. They'll want big enough premises, a reliable van etc, etc...

**On the
other
hand...**

...they will try to keep their spending on working capital to a minimum consistent with producing a quality product. They'll want to use as little material, time and overheads on each job as possible - and they'll want to sell their furniture - their finished stocks - for as much as possible.

The difference between what it costs to make their furniture and what they get when they sell it is called PROFIT. If they sell their furniture for cash they will end up with more money, which they can re-invest in fixed assets, or more materials, time and overheads to make the job.

Working Capital goes round in a circle

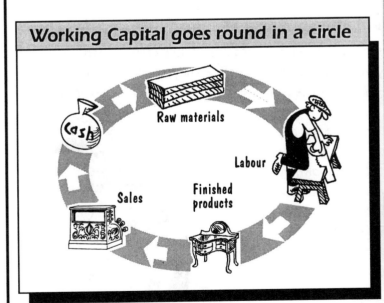

Successful businesses sell their goods for more than it costs to produce them, so the WORKING CAPITAL CYCLE will always make money.

This is how a business makes a profit.

Eventually that profit will turn into cash - but how profitable the business is depends on how long this process takes, because...

The hidden ingredient of the working capital cycle is ...

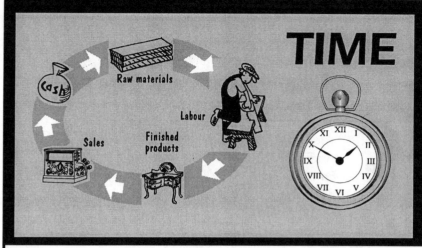

TIME

For a company to make a profit, the money in the working capital cycle must increase; but the amount of money depends on the speed at which that money moves. You can make *more* profit, but have to invest *less* money, by *speeding up* the working capital cycle.

Two outside factors affect the speed of the working capital cycle:

Creditors and Debtors

"An early settlement would be appreciated'

Creditors are people or organisations to whom the business owes money. They are most often suppliers of the materials that go into the things the business produces, although, of course, they supply fixed assets too.

Debtors are people or organisations who owe the business money, usually because they have bought the things the business produces.

'Put this on my account'

Creditors and debtors affect the speed of the working capital cycle

Creditors have the effect of allowing the working capital to speed up because, with customers who have accounts, they allow time to elapse before they ask for payment. So, for perhaps thirty days - sometimes longer - the business can trade using money it owes to its creditors.

Debtors have the opposite effect. They slow the working capital cycle down by delaying payment for the goods or services they have received, and on which the business has already spent money on producing and selling.

1

The balance sheet is a "snapshot" of the business's finance at a point of time. It tells you:
- where the money in a business comes from;
- where the money is invested in the business.

2

Companies invest money in two kinds of assets:
- fixed assets: things they mean to keep;
- working capital: things they mean to sell.

They also spend money on administrative overheads (admin costs), which are not assets.

3

Companies obtain money from
- shareholders, who provide share capital
- lenders; bankers and others, who provide loan capital.

4

Shareholders are paid dividends and own the company. If the company grows, they prosper. If it declines, they lose their money.

5

Lenders are paid interest and expect the loan to be repaid, whatever happens to the company.

6

Creditors are people to whom the business owes money. Debtors are people who owe the company money. They are part of working capital.

7

Successful companies sell goods for more than it costs to produce them, so the working capital cycle should always make money. But it takes time to turn it all into cash.

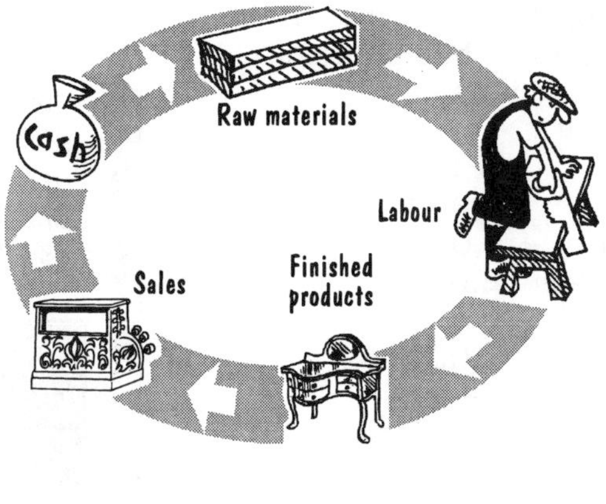

The working capital cycle gives a simplified view of what goes on in the real business of running a company. For example, it does not allow for unsold goods or work in progress - which also represents money tied up in working capital. But meanwhile the company has been set up and is ready to operate. Financially, how does it look at this stage?

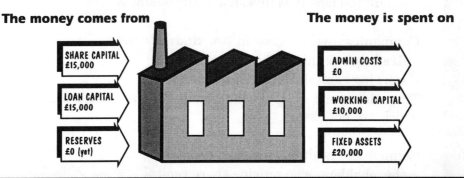

The money comes from

SHARE CAPITAL £15,000

LOAN CAPITAL £15,000

RESERVES £0 (yet)

The money is spent on

ADMIN COSTS £0

WORKING CAPITAL £10,000

FIXED ASSETS £20,000

If we were to make up a **balance sheet** of this situation, the 'snapshot' of Monday morning on the first month would look like this:

The money comes from		The money is invested in	
	£		£
Share capital	15,000	Fixed Assets	20,000
Loan capital	15,000	Working Capital	10,000
Reserves	0		
Total	£ 30,000	Total	£ 30,000

On Monday morning of the first month the company had £10,000 cash, but during the month it will spend it on:

	£
Stocks of wood	4,000
Factory wages	3,000
Factory overheads (power, light etc)	2,000
Admin costs	1,000
Total	£ 10,000

The working capital is represented by the stocks the company has already bought to start trading plus the amount of money it will need to produce and sell its furniture during the month.

Now let's look at the situation at the end of the month, after they have sold all they have produced.

The snapshot now looks like this:

The money comes from	£		The money is invested in	£
Share capital	15,000			
Loan capital	15,000		Fixed Assets	20,000
Reserves	0		Working Capital	11,000
Profit	1,000			
Total	£ 31,000		Total	£ 31,000

They've made a profit of £1,000. But how did they do that - and what does the £11,000 of working capital represent? They sold all their stock of furniture for £11,000, so **their working capital went up by £1,000**, from £10,000 to £11,000. Since they sold it for cash, all the working capital is cash...until the first Monday of the next month, when it will start disappearing again to purchase more materials, etc.

It *must* balance

Notice that the balance sheet always balances. A change on one side is always accompanied by a change (or changes) of the same amount on the other.
If it does not then either some assets are missing or there's some mistake in the accountancy.

The money comes from	£		The money is invested in	£
Share capital	15,000			
Loan capital	15,000		Fixed Assets	20,000
Reserves	0		Working Capital	5,000
(Profit)	(5,000)			
Total	£ 25,000		Total	£ 25,000

(Profit) in brackets = Loss!

If the company had sold its furniture stock for only £5,000 instead of £10,000 they would have made a loss of £5,000. The balance sheet would tell the story - but it would still **balance.**

13

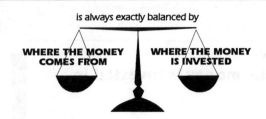

is always exactly balanced by

WHERE THE MONEY COMES FROM

WHERE THE MONEY IS INVESTED

So, by reading the balance sheet we can see where the business's money comes from and where it is invested. Now what about that other question on page 3?

How is the business doing?

Although profit and loss statements are traditionally prepared annually, there is no reason they couldn't appear more frequently. Some managing directors seem keen to have them as often as their financial department can produce them.

KEEP 'EM COMING!

What would our business's profit and loss statement look like at the end of the first month's trading?

Profit and Loss Statement

How the money has grown or shrunk through trading

The Profit and Loss Statement is the second important piece of financial information. It will tell us what trade the business has done over the period (usually a year.)

Fine Furniture Ltd Profit and Loss Statement for the month ending July 31st 19....		
		£
Sales		11,000
Cost of Sales	£	
Materials	4,000	
Wages	3,000	
Factory overheads	2,000	
Total	9,000	9,000
Gross Profit		2,000
Admin costs		1,000
Net Profit		£1,000

Notice there are two kinds of profit on this statement - Gross and Net. **Gross** profit is simply sales less cost of producing the furniture. These costs are equal to the working capital before selling the furniture. **Net** profit is after admin costs have been taken out. Any interest on loans and shareholders' dividends will be paid out of **net profit,** and anything over is called **retained profit** which will go to increasing the reserves of the company (see page 6) and will be shown on the balance sheet. Admin costs will come out of the reserves at the end of the first month.

Profit and loss statements can tell you roughly how your business is doing at any given time. But there are some things they can't do.

1 If you have any spare cash

You can make a profit and still have no cash. Making a profit means that all the assets in the company have grown, but not that you have available cash - your working capital cycle may have slowed, or you could have bought some new equipment; so you may be short of cash - but it won't show in your P/L statement.

2 How well the company is actually doing

Simply because you are making a profit doesn't mean you are doing well. If you make a profit of £50,000 from a capital investment of £2.5 million you would have been better off investing in a building society. The P/L statement doesn't tell you about capital investment - for that you'd have to read the balance sheet as well.

3 Anything about profit on individual product lines

The P/L statement normally amalgamates information from all your product lines. To find out more you would have to delve into individual product costings.

4 What you need to know to make financial decisions

The P/L statement covers only one trading period. It is important to see the trend - whether profits are going up or down. Trends give you advance warning of dangers. But trends will only give you an indication of what will happen in the future if things continue as they have in the past. What you need to do is to look at each sales and expense category individually in the light of your marketing and production plans for the future, and budget for each one. You can't plan on the basis of one P/L statement

5 An exact figure

The measurement of profit and loss is affected by many factors, like whether you will judge a long-term debt to be a bad (i.e. irrecoverable) debt, or whether sums put aside to buy new equipment (see depreciation, p 18) are adequate. Judgements are made about whether stocks are obsolete or unsaleable. All these will affect figures in the P/L statement.

SO WHAT DOES A PROFIT AND LOSS STATEMENT TELL YOU?

It tells you how the trading performance of the company has caused the assets of the business to grow - or shrink.
But profit is not cash, and it is only one part of the information you need to run a business. Use it with information on balance sheets and with what you know of your cash flow situation to make your budgets for the future.

HOW DEBTORS AFFECT THE COMPANY'S ACCOUNTS

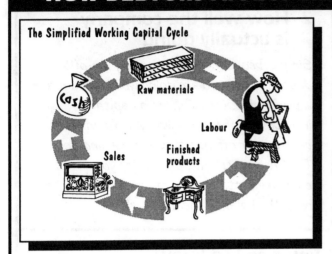

The Simplified Working Capital Cycle

Cash — Raw materials — Labour — Finished products — Sales

The elements that make up the trading activities - i.e., the cost of sales - of a company are contained in the working capital cycle. We've already seen a simplified version of it, and we've seen that there are other elements whch speed up or slow down the working of the cycle, like creditors and debtors. What happens to the balance sheet and profit and loss statement if, say, Fine Furniture's customer delayed payment by a month?

The money comes from

	£
Share capital	15,000
Loan capital	15,000
Reserves	0
Profit	1,000
Total	£ 31,000

The money is invested in

	£
Fixed Assets	20,000
Working Capital: Debtors	11,000
Total	£ 31,000

	£	
Sales (debtors)		**11,000**
to pay for	£	
Stocks	4,000	
Factory wages	3,000	
Factory o'hds	2,000	
Cost of sales	9,000	
Admin costs	1,000	10,000
Profit		£ 1,000

The only difference in the balance sheet is that the cash in the working capital is now represented by debtors; not much difference, you might think, until you try paying the wages or start replacing your stocks of wood...

The business has made its £1,000 profit, but it hasn't generated any additional cash at all, because PROFIT IS NOT CASH.

A profitable business can go bankrupt simply because it does not have enough cash to pay its bills.

Where is Jack's profit?

So, if profit is not cash, what is it?

Profit simply describes how the assets - any assets - grew through trading. It is **an entry on one side of the balance sheet describing where the money has been spent.**

So, profit could be in debtors, as we've seen. It could be in wood, if Jack had received cash for his sale and immediately gone out and bought stock. In the same way, if he had used the money to buy machinery, that's where some of his assets would lie. It could be anywhere in the assets of the balance sheet - including cash.

HOW CREDITORS AFFECT THE COMPANY'S ACCOUNTS

If Fine Furniture's customers don't pay up immediately, what will Jack do to meet his weekly bills?

He has two options for raising cash:

1 Credit from his suppliers

He can become a debtor himself, if his supplier will allow him to open an account. With luck he will be able to balance his debtor's time delay with one of his own.

2 A bank loan or overdraft

The bank will charge him interest on any money lent to the business, and will probably require some form of security.

Here's what the balance sheet would look like in each case

1 The company receives £4,000 credit from its suppliers

Although the money is, in effect, a loan, it does not form part of the company's loan capital. Instead it is shown as a minus item as part of the working capital.

The money comes from	£	The money is invested in	£
Share capital	15,000	Fixed Assets	20,000
Loan capital	15,000	Working Capital:	
Reserves	0	Stock	4,000
Profit	1,000	Debtors	11,000
		less Creditors	(4,000)
Total	£ 31,000	Total	£ 31,000

2 The company asks for a £4,000 loan/overdraft from the bank

This time the original sum of money the company has borrowed from the bank (or from another source) has been increased by £4,000, so is shown on the left hand side of the balance sheet.

The money comes from	£	The money is invested in	£
Share capital	15,000	Fixed Assets	20,000
Loan capital	19,000	Working Capital:	
Reserves	0	Stock	4,000
Profit	1,000	Debtors	11,000
Total	£ 35,000	Total	£ 35,000

Naturally, Jack would rather obtain free credit from his supplier rather than an interest-bearing loan from the bank; but whether this would be wise or not depends on how soon the debtor will pay up. Jack could be in trouble if he could not meet his supplier's bills on the due date.

Adding Creditors and Debtors to the working capital cycle

Speeding up the working capital cycle increases the company's profitability. You can do this by:

* keeping stock levels to a minimum
* delaying payment to creditors for as long as possible
* getting your debtors to pay up as soon as possible

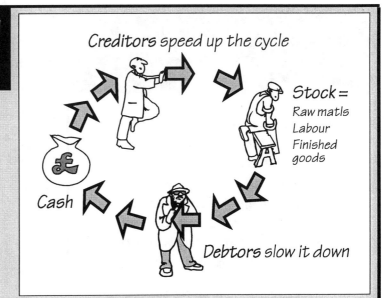

Creditors speed up the cycle

Stock = Raw matls Labour Finished goods

Cash

Debtors slow it down

Whilst Jack wants to keep working capital as low as he can, he will want the best fixed assets he can afford.

But even the best wear out eventually, and as they wear the assets of the company diminish. How does he account for his fixed assets losing their value?

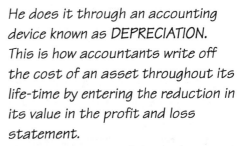

He does it through an accounting device known as DEPRECIATION. This is how accountants write off the cost of an asset throughout its life-time by entering the reduction in its value in the profit and loss statement.

The simplest way of doing this is called "straight line depreciation", which writes off the asset by equal amounts each year of its life.

Suppose all of Jack's fixed assets were estimated to last ten years. He could write off £2,000 each year until they had zero value at the end of year 10.

Diminishing "value" of fixed assets

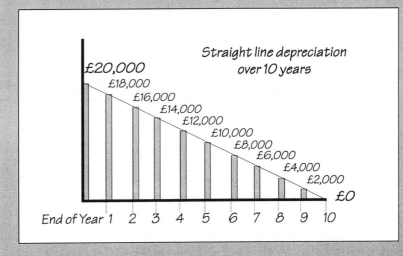

Straight line depreciation over 10 years

£20,000
£18,000
£16,000
£14,000
£12,000
£10,000
£8,000
£6,000
£4,000
£2,000
£0

End of Year 1 2 3 4 5 6 7 8 9 10

Showing depreciation on the Profit and Loss Statement and the Balance Sheet

When fixed assets are depreciated they affect the amount of money invested in the business, so they represent a cost to the business. The prudent manager will put the amount required to cover depreciation aside, so the money is still available for the business to use, should it need to.

In the balance sheet below, the amount shown against depreciation could eventually be turned into fixed assets as new equipment is bought to replace worn out items.

Fine Furniture Ltd
Profit and Loss Statement
for the month ending June 30th 19....

	£	£
Sales		11,000
Cost of Sales	£	
Materials	4,000	
Wages	3,000	
Factory O'hds	2,000	
Total	9,000	(9,000)
Gross Profit		2,000
less **Admin Costs**		(1,000)
		1,000
less **Depreciation**		(167)
Net Profit		£ 833

Fine Furniture took £200,000 in its first year of trading and made a profit of £12,000, before allowing for depreciation. Its first balance sheet looked like this:

The money comes from			The money is invested in		
		£			£
Share capital		15,000	Fixed Assets		20,000
Loan capital		15,000	less Deprec'n		(2,000)
Reserves		0			
Profit	12,000				18,000
less Deprc'n of 2,000		10,000			
			Working Capital		22,000
Total		£40,000			
			Total		£ 40,000

A crucial question is: how much of that working capital is cash? That depends on how good Jack is at managing his working capital cycle. He will need some cash to pay the interest on the £15,000 loan. And if he's really successful he might have some left over to pay a dividend to his shareholders.
In chapter 2 we'll see how he's really done.

Here's hoping!

1 The profit and loss statement tells you how the money has performed through trading over a period.

2 Profit simply describes how the assets of the business grew through trading.

3 Profit is not cash. You can make a profit and still have no cash.

4 By speeding up the working capital cycle - minimising stocks, getting debtors to pay up quickly, and by taking maximum credit, you need less money to invest in the business.

5 The cost of fixed assets is written off over their life using "depreciation".

3 Controlling Cash Flow

The business has been going for a year, and has proved to be a modest success. Jack and Andy have taken on more labour, both in the workshop and in the office, because the firm has landed a big contract to supply Deal's the Furnishers with bedroom furniture. Jack looks at his balance sheet with satisfaction.

Making plans for meeting the increased workload has implications for the company's working capital and fixed assets, and both Jack and Andy are busy taking the necessary steps.

The business is in profit, so they can afford to spend some money on labour, materials and equipment...

I've allowed for the new cabinet makers

Don't forget we'll need another lathe

...and there will be decisions to be made about the amount of space needed to make and store the extra stock...

Mail, Mr Plank

But the postman is the bearer of bad news

Dear Mr Plank,

Your current account is now considerably overdrawn. As you have no overdraft facility with this bank, I would request that you make arrangements to repay the outstanding amount immediately.

Yours sincerely

Attila T. Hun

Manager, Southern Bank Ltd

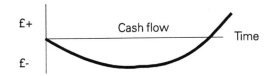
Poor Jack

A guest at the table is Jack's cousin Vivienne, the Finance Director of United Industries, a very large company.

She is sympathetic - and helpful. But first she scares the living daylights out of him.

I'm afraid you are in the Death Valley Curve!

It's like this:

When you start trading you have to spend money on making and selling your goods before you have a chance to get any back through sales. During that time you will have a negative cash flow.

This is fine if you can afford to trade all that time without any money coming in - it doesn't matter so much if your customers pay up immediately, and if you don't have to expand to meet demand. But if you suddenly get a big order...

...it might be ages before you finished making your goods, and longer still to get paid. You could have a profit on paper, but go out of business waiting for your money.

£+

Cash flow

Time

£-

Death Valley

Doomed! I'll never find the cash to repay my overdraft! Scuppered by my petty greed!

"It's called the Death Valley Curve. Many successful businesses have gone bust in Death Valley, because they overtraded, that is, they took on more business than they could cope with. You can overtrade at any time in the business's life - you don't have to be a new business to fall into this trap. And Jack, you have overtraded, I'm afraid."

Oh, you're not all that doomed, Jack. I'll come to the factory and help you tomorrow. Meanwhile, what's for pudding?

Next day...

"Your order book's fantastic, so we'll get the bank to give you an overdraft. With this kind of business in hand you'll have no trouble, but they'll want some kind of security; and it's better to go to them before they come to you, as they did this time. We call it Cash Flow Planning."

March **April**

M	T	W	T	F	S	S		F	S	S
1	2	3	4	5	6	7		2	3	4
8	9	10	11	12	13	14		9	10	11
15	16	17	18	19	20	21		16	17	18
22	23	24	25	26	27	28		23	24	25
29	30	31						30		

"To show what I mean. look at this first order. You've arranged to start making it on March 1st, for delivery at the end of the following week, on the 12th, but I bet your customer won't settle the bill until six weeks later. Meanwhile you have to go on trading without any cash coming in."

"And your second order is going to make things worse. You'll start it on the 9th of March, for completion on the 23rd, but unless you are firm with your client you probably won't see that money until the end of April either - which means that you'd better find some cash from somewhere to trade throughout April.

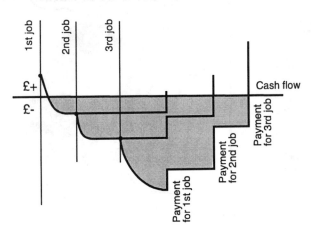

But what about the work we've done, and the invoices we've already sent out?

That's a recipe for disaster, Jack!

"Relying on money which you are owed, but which has not come in yet, could result in bankruptcy! A better bet would be a bank loan, or perhaps you could farm the work out. Sooner or later you'll have some reserves to tide you over, but first, look at what's happening to your cash flow....

This is how Death Valley gets deeper and deeper...

"Fine Furniture's profitability grows with every job - but only if it can survive cash flow's Death Valley Curve.

Look what happens when you take on three jobs before you have been paid for the first one: Death Valley gets deeper and deeper until the first payment comes in, and gets shallower and shallower by steps as the other jobs gets paid for.

You have to survive that period somehow - so you'd better keep a record of your cash flow so that you can plan ahead."

My **cash book** keeps a record of all my **cash** outgoings and all my **cash** income...

CASH BOOK

Date	Item	Details	Out	In	Balance (7381.96)
	Balance	Brought forward from March			(9482.53)
April			2100.57		
2	Wages	Staff	2100.57		
	Weekly total		10.00		
5	Stationery	Petty cash	243.71		
5	Elect. bill	Electricity Co Ltd	173.20		
7	Petrol account	Garage	365.12		(12375.13)
9	Busnss Rates	Local Authority	2100.57		
9	Wages	Staff	2892.60		
	Weekly total		2455.74		(16931.44)
12	Stock	Bark & Son	2100.57		
16	Wages	Staff	4556.31		
	Weekly total		2204.89		
19	Stock	Bark & Son	2100.57	16578.39	(353.05)
23	Wages	Staff		16578.39	
23	Payment	Deals	4305.46		
	Weekly total				

Yes, but it would have to be modified if you want it to be a **forecast** - I'll show you later.

Mind you, that right hand column **does** show how deep you are in **Death Valley**

The Cash Flow Forecast will tell you how much cash you will need to carry on trading. But even in your cash book you can see that the bills keep on coming in relentlessly whether you are trading or not, and that when you do trade, the cost of buying stock bumps up the cash flow defecit significantly. To cope with all this, until you are paid and paid again, you need a reservoir of cash - and if you don't have it you will need an adequate bank loan.

A third of businesses that fail do so within three years of starting up

This is mostly because they are under-capitalised to start with. They never come out of Death Valley alive.

Vivienne continues her tour of inspection

Let's take a look around. Something tells me overtrading isn't your only problem.

Creditors speed up the cycle

Stock =
Raw materials
Labour
Finished goods

Cash

Debtors slow it down

For instance, there are some items in the working capital cycle that could repay our attention...

Take the matter of debtors, for example

Put this lot on account, old mate

Er...OK

You will need to be much stricter about giving credit. You'll have to work out some system of credit control which will be acceptable to your customers but will protect you from unscrupulous opportunists.

GOLDEN RULES...

**Choose your customers with care,
Set credit limits,
Speed up payments**

Choosing your customers	Setting credit limits	Speeding up payments
✔ Ask for, and check up on, trade references ✔ Ask for bank references ✔ Make credit checks with other suppliers ✔ Read any published information about the customer's firm ✔ Make sales visits to his/her premises	 When you have checked your customer's references you can offer him/her a monthly credit ceiling. This will minimise the risk you are taking.	There are a number of inducements - and threats - you can offer your customers to make them pay up promptly... 

If all that fails - and even if it doesn't, you can try phoning to ask if your invoice or the customer's cheque has perhaps gone astray. You could refer to your company's policy of discounts for prompt payments (if it has one). You can explain it is the end of the financial year/VAT period; or you could just ask for the money. If you are in the process of producing another order for the same customer you are in a particularly strong position, because you can point out that you do not have the funds to continue...etc

Sometimes you can get part of the payment in advance. For instance, if you land a contract to supply large value items which will involve you in considerable outlay, it is sometimes possible to ask for a proportion of the cost "up front". This practice is common amongst video production companies, who when bidding for work stipulate one third on signing the contract, one third at an intermediate point and the remainder on completion. This depends on the state of the market, and what your competitors are asking; but if the overall price is acceptable to the client it is likely that he/she will be willing to pay in stages.

Tight control of cash flow is essential if you want to stay in business

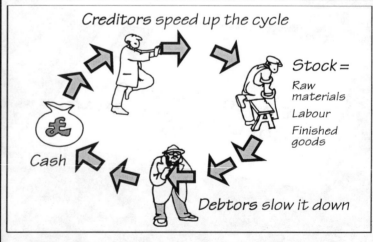

Another area of the working capital cycle which can help your cash flow is in your dealings with creditors

A good relationship with your creditors is important for the success of the business

They can be your suppliers, your bank manager, HM Customs and Excise (the VATman), the Inland Revenue...

In fact, anyone to whom you owe money. But it isn't a good idea to be constantly chased by your creditors, who are in a position to refuse credit or call in unsecured loans when they feel like it.

Golden Rule: Make an arrangement and stick to it

...so the vital element in good relations with your creditors is to get a good deal at the beginning. You won't get credit just by asking, although no-one will give it if you don't. Suppliers will need bank and trade references before they will perform services or let their goods go without immediate payment.

Bark & Sons Timber Merchants
7 Plane Tree Drive Woodmanstern

STATEMENT to *Fine Furniture*
Date *April 30th 19—*

Invoice No	Date	£ Net	£ VAT	£ Total
7621	22/3	2330.54	407.84	2738.38
7739	28/3	1763.78	308.66	2072.44
8412	12/4	1045.00	182.87	1227.87
8954	19/4	1876.50	328.39	2204.89
Total £		7015.82	1227.76	8243.58
Total 30 days		2921.50	511.26	3432.76
Total due now		4094.32	716.50	4810.82

A good credit arrangement. Notice how, at the foot of this monthly statement, the supplier is asking for only part of the bill to be paid now. That is because two of the four invoices fall within the 30-day credit allowed his customer.

Keep your bank informed of your progress

They are as keen for you to succeed as you are, because they prefer to have successful customers, particularly if they have lent you money. They will be reassured by a full order book, but they will be happier still if they see an intelligent cash flow forecast. So, if it's only for the bank's sake, try to avoid overtrading. In any case, the most likely organisation to put you into liquidation won't be the bank...

...it's more likely to be the Inland Revenue or the Customs and Excise Department, neither of which have a vested interest in your success - only in claiming the money that is legally due to them.

So, when dealing with creditors:

Agree good terms with your supplier

Don't pay early

Try for part payment on large orders until you get paid

Keep the bank informed

Remember you have to pay tax

Meanwhile...

You have been tying cash up for **months!** Here's another way you can improve your cash flow situation - better stock control

"It makes absolutely no sense to tie up capital like this. Thousands of pounds worth of timber which could be earning interest as savings in the bank, and it's just lying here. The point is, buy only what you need when you need it. Your supplier isn't a hundred miles away! Aim to buy only what you need for your work in progress.

"I am afraid you are going to have to do much more homework before you buy stock. Accuracy saves money."

...and don't forget that other important ingredient in the working capital cycle - LABOUR

Don't interrupt them unless you really have to - they are assets only when they are working

"...they are as important as stock to the health of your cash flow. In fact, all the components of the working capital cycle - creditors, debtors, labour, raw materials, finished goods - have an effect on the amount of cash you have available to trade. When you've got all this right we can start looking at the business properly, and analysing how we can make it more profitable."

Golden rules about stock control

Buy only what you need now

but buy at the beginning of the month to increase credit time

Buy in small quantities

Don't interrupt production runs unless it's really worth it

Only make to order, if possible

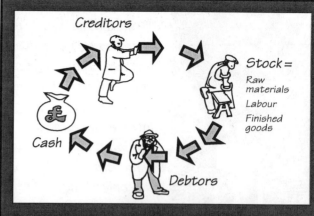

Creditors

Cash

Debtors

Stock =
Raw materials
Labour
Finished goods

You've been working hard for a year: the business looks healthy on paper but you are short of cash. Your business needs, in the short term, to solve its cash flow problem, and in the long term, to go in for some financial planning.

You can effect some savings in the working capital area by paying more attention to your debtors, creditors and stock...

..and you can try solving your immediate cash flow problem either by getting a bank loan or overdraft - but this will put a hole in your profits because you'll have to pay quite high interest rates...

or you could perhaps sub-contract part of your work to other firms. Once again, you would be losing profit, but getting other companies to take on some of the jobs would transfer part of the cash flow problem to them - and you wouldn't need to expand your production base temporarily to cope with a short term problem.

And you are going to have to upgrade your office procedures to handle your accounts more efficiently.

But your business isn't going to be really successful unless you plan for the future - say the next three years - and prepare financial budgets which are attainable and which don't rely on luck or guesswork. Luckily you will have heard of the key financial tools you will need - the profit and loss forecast, the cash flow forecast and the balance sheet forecast.

Planning for success will take a little time, but it's crucial if you are going to build this company up into a successful organisation.

PROFIT AND LOSS FORECAST

CASH FLOW FORECAST

BALANCE SHEET FORECAST

In chapter 4 we'll begin by _forecasting performance_...

3 Summary

1   Profit is not the same as cash. You can be profitable and still run out of cash.

2   Beware Death Valley! When you start-up or expand your business, you can use far more cash than you expect - or have available. It takes time to sell stocks and time for debtors to pay up; so you need to manage your working capital.

3   You can speed up the collection of debts by:
- choosing your customers carefully
- setting appropriate credit limits
- taking the right measures to speed up payments

4   Handle your creditors carefully. If you make an arrangement, stick to it. Remember to
- agree good terms
- try for part payment on large orders
- don't pay early
- keep the bank informed
- pay your taxes

5   You can minimise your stock holding by:
- buying only what you need now
- buying at the beginning of the month
- buying small quantities
- not interrupting production runs
- only making to order, if possible

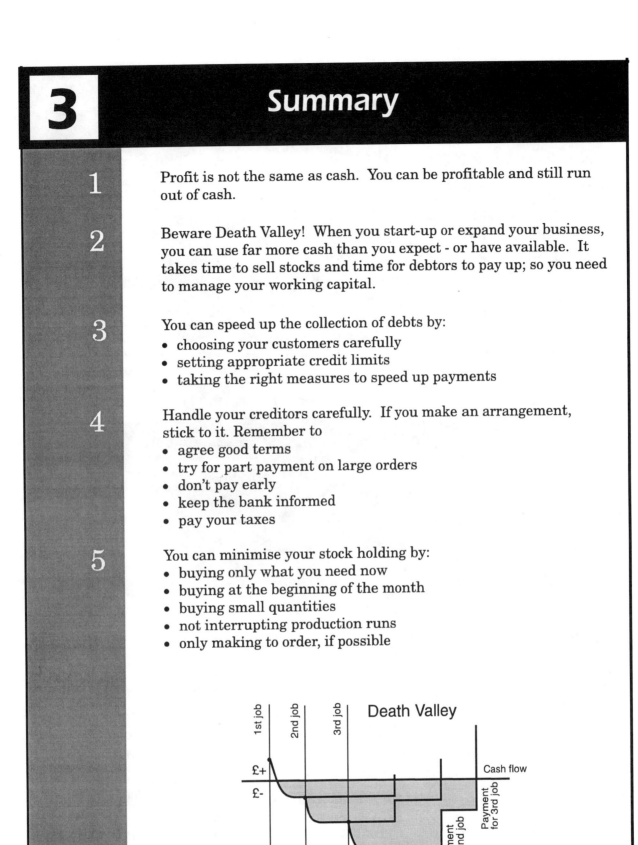

4 Forecasting Performance

According to my Work in Progress book, our customers have placed orders totalling £150,000...

That will take about £60,000 of materials - but I think we ought to buy a bit more, just in case...let's say £100,000 worth

Factory wages for six months will amount to around £42,000... and then overheads are working out at £6,000 per month - that's £36,000

So what's going to happen in the next six months, Andy?

Let's see what we've got lined up

And we must not forget to put aside a sum to take account of the depreciation of our capital assets, to quote Vivienne

Sales	150,000
Materials in sales	60,000
Labour in sales	42,000
Overheads	36,000
Depreciation	1,000

	£	£
Sales		150,000
Materials in sales	60,000	
Labour in sales	42,000	
Overheads	36,000	
Depreciation	1,000	
	139,000	139,000
Profit £		11,000

It looks as if we'll be doing quite well six months from now - same profit as the **whole** of last year*

Maybe. On past experience we'll get about £120,000 of that £150,000 paid on time. More to the point, we need a new lathe - and that will cost £10,000

*p20

Jack and Andy have prepared a Profit and Loss Forecast for the next six months. In reality, businesses prepare forecasts for longer periods - up to three years - and for more complex patterns of trading.

In even the shortest accounting period most businesses sell more than one product to more than one customer, and this diagram illustrates a more realistic situation.

Products/Services

	Existing	New
Existing	Base Forecast	Growth Forecast 2
New	Growth Forecast 1	Growth Forecast 3

Markets

All businesses have existing products or services, and many have new ones to offer their customers. At the same time, all businesses have existing customers, and most want new ones. So it is certain that they will sell existing products or services to existing customers, while it is probable that, to a greater or lesser extent, they will have combinations of new and existing products/services and customers as shown. This means four different forecasts.

The base forecast will be the easiest and most accurate to calculate. If your business depends on a high level of repeat orders you can build your forecast on your existing customers: if you rely on impulse buying, look at the overall level of sales and how it might be affected by market trends.

Start the budgeting process with Existing Products/Services for Existing Markets/Customers and ask yourself...

What was your level of sales last year?

Will your customers continue to buy your products or services?

Can you therefore rely on the same level of sales as last year?

Your own performance will be affected by market trends, the state of the business environment and by competition.

Conduct a S.W.O.T. Analysis to find out your company's STRENGTHS and WEAKNESSES, and the OPPORTUNITIES and THREATS presented by the market place.

What is a SWOT Analysis?

Two pieces of research: an investigation (or audit) into the kind of a company you are and another into the business environment you operate in.

A number of features - e.g. the particular talents of individuals, the firm's financial standing, the way the company has developed over a period, may give it some unique strengths or weaknesses, which can be revealed by an **internal audit.**

Similarly, elements in the business environment - the degree of competition, government legislation, the economic climate etc will give the business an idea of the threats and opportunities confronting it - revealed by an **external audit**.

A SWOT Analysis will give you valuable information which you can use in your Growth Forecasts

...but the more unfamiliar the territory, the less accurate will be your forecasts

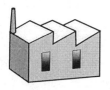

Base Forecast

Growth Forecast 1

Growth Forecast 2

Growth Forecast 3

The business will have to forecast its profitability in three areas where accuracy becomes increasingly difficult

With existing products/services and existing markets it can rely on existing information

It will have to invest in more production, sales staff, advertising to cope with these areas

In this uncharted area it will have to rely on expensive market research, guesswork and luck

Estimating sales is never easy, but sales estimates are the foundation on which the rest of the budget is built. The following check list should help you compile your sales forecast.

SALES FORECAST CHECKLIST

Base Forecast

✓ What were sales last year?

✓ Will your product range change (in terms of quality of product etc)?

✓ Is the price of your product/service going to increase?

✓ Do you expect the same level of repeat sales next year?

✓ Will advertising expenditure change this year?

✓ Do you expect to generate the same level of new enquiries as last year?

✓ Do you intend to increase your sales force?

✓ Will targets for your sales force change?

✓ Do you expect the conversion rate (from enquiry to sale) to change?

✓ Do your competitors have plans that might affect you?

New Markets

✓ Can you estimate sales based on experience of existing customers?

✓ Will your new sales force perform as efficiently as your old?

✓ Will you generate the same level of enquiries as in your existing markets?

✓ Will you have the same conversion rates as in your existing markets?

✓ What competition do you face in your new markets, compared to your old ones?

New Products or Services

✓ Can your existing customers give you an estimate of sales?

✓ Can your sales force give you an estimate of sales?

✓ Can you judge sales from your competitors' products/services?

✓ Are there any other "experts" in the area who could advise you?

✓ Is the product/service likely to be price-sensitive?

✓ If you are introducing a new product or service into a new market, are you certain that the risks are acceptable?

Profit & Loss Forecast for 6months from Jan....

	£	£
Sales	£	150,000
Materials in sales	60,000	
Labour in sales	42,000	
Overheads	36,000	
Depreciation	1,000	
	139,000	139,000
Profit £		11,000

Remember Fine Furniture's 6-month P/L forecast looked like this

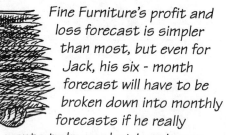

Fine Furniture's profit and loss forecast is simpler than most, but even for Jack, his six - month forecast will have to be broken down into monthly forecasts if he really wants to know what is going on financially and get early warning of future crises.

Monthly Profit & Loss forecast from Jan to June

	MONTH 1	2	3	4	5	6	Total
Sales	12,500	12,500	17,500	30,000	37,500	40,000	150,000
less							
Mat'ls in sales	(5,000)	(5,000)	(7,000)	(12,000)	(15,000)	(16,000)	(60,000)
Labour in sales	(3,000)	(3,000)	(6,000)	(9,000)	(10,000)	(11,000)	(42,000)
Overheads	(4,000)	(4,000)	(4,000)	(6,000)	(9,000)	(9,000)	(36,000)
Profit	500	500	500	3,000	3,500	4,000	12,000
Deprec'n							1,000
Profit (Loss) £							11,000

This is OK as far as it goes - sales for one month give you an idea of cash coming in the next month...

...but it will tell you nothing about your **accumulated** cash situation from month to month

So now, you have to make a cash flow forecast for the same period.

Call me when you've done it.... And - good luck!

But remember the balance sheet at the end of the first year (p20)?

The working capital of £22,000 hid a considerable amount of debt. When broken down, it looked like this:

Stocks of wood	24,000
Debtors	10,000
less	
Creditors	(2,000)
Overdraft	(10,000)
	22,000

The money comes from

	£	
Share capital		15,000
Loan capital		15,000
Reserves		0
Profit	12,000	
less Deprc'n of 2,000		10,000
Total		£40,000

The money is invested in

	£	
Fixed Assets		20,000
less Deprec'n		(2,000)
		18,000
Working Capital		22,000
Total		£ 40,000

No wonder the bank was so concerned (p22).

Jack is just about to make his cash flow forecast. What will it reveal?

And so...

Eventually he is obliged to seek Vivienne's advice

Sales Receipts	
Total (A)	
Payments	
Raw materials	
Employee wages & NI	
Overheads	
Fixed Assets	
Total (B)	
Balances	
Cash increase (dec.) (A)-(B)	
Opening balance	
Closing balance	

You need a proper cash flow forecast. I will fax you an example...

Help!

Jack embarks on the task of designing a cash flow forecast which will be realistic, and he finds it difficult to know what to put in. A voice in his ear keeps saying "everything", but he realises that's impossible.

I have made three sections: Sales, Payments and Balances. The Balances will show the difference in the totals between A and B.

CASH FLOW FORECAST — MONTH 1 2 3 4 5 6 TOTAL

Sales Receipts / Total (A) / Payments / Raw materials / Employee wages / Overheads / Fixed Assets / Total B / Balances / Cash Increase (dec.) (A)-(B) / Opening balance / Closing balance

Again, you'll have to fill it in every month for six months.

You may want to add a few items to total B like the monthly repayments of your bank loan...

... or if you borrow money the amount of the loan goes into total A since it's cash coming in

I can see that the balances will tell me how far into Death Valley I'm getting

And this is the cash flow forecast Jack came up with...

CASH FLOW FORECAST	MONTH						
	1	2	3	4	5	6	TOTAL
Sales Receipts	10,000	12,500	12,500	17,500	30,000	37,500	120,000
Total (A)	10,000	12,500	12,500	17,500	30,000	37,500	120,000
Payments							
Raw materials	15,000	15,000	5,000	5,000	5,000	5,000	50,000
Employee wages	7,000	7,000	7,000	7,000	7,000	7,000	42,000
Overheads	6,000	6,000	6,000	6,000	6,000	6,000	36,000
Fixed Assets	10,000						10,000
Total B	38,000	28,000	18,000	18,000	18,000	18,000	138,000
Balances							
Cash Increase (dec.) (A)-(B)	(28,000)	(15,500)	(5,500)	(500)	12,000	19,500	(18,000)
Opening balance	(10,000)	(38,000)	(53,500)	(59,000)	(59,500)	(47,500)	(10,000)
Closing balance	(38,000)	(53,500)	(59,000)	(59,500)	(47,500)	(28,000)	(28,000)

Oh no!

Jack, this will **not do!** You'll never be able to borrow £59,500. You've already got a loan of £15,000 and the bank doesn't even want to let you keep an overdraft of £10,000. You'll have to do **something!**

Gulp!

Jack's cash flow forecast arrives on Vivienne's fax machine

Look, Jack, try to remember last year's balance sheet...

The money comes from		£	The money is invested in		£
Share capital		15,000	Fixed Assets		20,000
Loan capital		15,000	*less* Deprec'n		(2,000)
Reserves		0			
Profit	12,000				18,000
less Deprc'n of 2,000		10,000			
			Working Capital		22,000
Total		£40,000			
			Total		£ 40,000

	£
Stocks	24,000
Debtors	10,000
less	
Creditors	(2,000)
Overdraft	(10,000)
Total	£ 22,000

"What about all that stock of timber I saw when I looked around? That balance sheet from your first year's trading showed that you had stocks of £24,000 - that's 2½ months' worth of sales on your current projection. With that much stock you won't need to buy £60,000 worth of raw materials to achieve your estimated sales of £150,000*. You'll only need to buy, say, £50,000 worth."

*See the P/L forecast on p36.

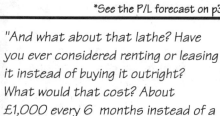

What's more, you could delay payment for a month and in the period you'd end up paying out only about £35,000 for stock.

That would cut your cash expenditures.

"And what about that lathe? Have you ever considered renting or leasing it instead of buying it outright? What would that cost? About £1,000 every 6 months instead of a big expenditure of £10,000 all at once."

FOR SALE OR LEASE

I think you and Andy had better have another go. Fax it to me - any time will do.

CASH FLOW FORECAST	MONTH						
	1	2	3	4	5	6	TOTAL
Sales Receipts	10,000	12,500	12,500	17,500	30,000	37,500	120,000
Total (A)	10,000	12,500	12,500	17,500	30,000	37,500	120,000
Payments							
Raw materials	2,500	2,500	5,000	5,000	10,000	10,000	35,000
Employee wages	7,000	7,000	7,000	7,000	7,000	7,000	42,000
Overheads	6,000	6,000	6,000	6,000	6,000	6,000	36,000
Rent of lathe	1,000						1,000
Total B	16,500	15,500	18,000	18,000	23,000	23,000	114,000
Balances							
Cash Increase (dec.) (A)-(B)	(6,500)	(3,000)	(5,500)	(500)	7,000	14,500	6,000
Opening balance	(10,000)	(16,500)	(19,500)	(25,000)	(25,500)	(18,500)	(10,000)
Closing balance	(16,500)	(19,500)	(25,000)	(25,500)	(18,500)	(4,000)	(4,000)

Here comes the best I can do. Hope you weren't in bed, or anything.

I don't think it's all that wonderful - we'll need an overdraft of £25,500 in month 4

Still, it'll be down to £4000 by month 6. But the lathe took our profits down by £1,000 to £10,000

Oy, that was quick! Yes, this cash flow forecast looks better, Jack.

"You can go to your bank manager and show him that you intend to reduce the overdraft in 6 months time. he should give you an overdraft of £26,000 for the two months you need it - provided you can give him some collateral or a personal guarantee. Yes, this cash flow forecast is certainly a lot better than the first one, which was a recipe for bankruptcy!"

Now prepare a balance sheet forecast. You have all the information at your disposal - what you spent on fixed assets, depreciation, working capital figures, debtors and creditors...

Oh NO! What do I need to do that for?

43

Jack found a lot of the information he wanted in the previous balance sheet (at the end of the first year)

Jack knew that his share capital was unchanged (no more money from auntie)...

...that he still owed this to the bank

...and this profit is carried forward as reserves

The money comes from		£
Share capital		15,000
Loan capital		15,000
Reserves		0
Profit	12,000	
less Deprc'n of 2,000		10,000
Total		£40,000

The money is invested in	£
Fixed Assets	20,000
less Deprec'n	(2,000)
	18,000
Working Capital	22,000
Total	£ 40,000

This fixed assets figure will depreciate by a further £1,000 in the first six months of the 2nd year

Jack's calculation

He knew he had to balance the money coming into the company with the money invested in working capital and fixed assets.

The money came in from shareholders, from loans, from his profit and from the reserves that had been accumulated from the profits of previous trading.

On the investment side of the balance sheet he carried forward the fixed assets sum from the previous year. Then he looked at the working capital. He calculated the amount of stock, debtors and creditors he had. The cash flow forecast had told him that he would have an overdraft of £4,000. And, of course, thanks to the hire of the lathe, his profit was down by £1,000 to £10,000.

Jack's Working Capital

Stock

Stock brought forward	£24,000
Stock purchased	50,000
	74,000
Cost of sales	(60,000)
Stock at end of period	14,000

Debtors

Debtors brought forward	£10,000
Sales	150,000
	160,000
Payments received	(120,000)
Debtors at end of period	40,000

Creditors

Stock creditors brought fwd	(£2,000)
Stock purchased	(50,000)
	(52,000)
Payments for stock	35,000
Creditors at end of period	(17,000)

And he came up with...

Projected Balance Sheet as at 30 June

Where the money comes from

	£	
Share capital		15,000
Loan capital		15,000
Reserves:	£	
brought forward	10,000	
profit for 6 months	10,000	20,000
Capital employed		50,000

I'm glad you agreed to put that in. It's the sum of all your capital

I don't see the point yet but I have a feeling I will

Where the money is invested

Fixed assets:	£	£	£
Costs	18,000		
less depreciation	(1,000)		17,000
Working capital			
Current assets			
Stocks	14,000		
Debtors	40,000	54,000	
less			
Current liabilities			
Creditors	(17,000)		
Overdraft	(4,000)	(21,000)	33,000
Net assets			50,000

Next day - Jack visits the bank

I trust you have brought your financial forecasts, Mr Plank

...hmm...making £10,000 on £50,000 of capital ...return on capital of 20% over six months, that's 40% over the year ..... hmm ... hmm.....trading pattern .. liabilities... stock levels ...hmm ... outstanding loan ...

Well, Mr Plank, you've got your overdraft. Your company is in quite good shape, isn't it? We'll be pleased to do business with you!

?

I still don't get it

Buy me a coffee and you will

(In the next chapter)

1 You must prepare a cash flow forecast. Try a few "what if?" questions to see the effect of different actions on your cash flow.

2 The cash flow forecast tells you how much cash you have - or need to borrow.

3 The profit and loss forecast tells you how much the business will grow - how its assets will increase - through trading.

4 The balance sheet forecast tells you what assets you will have and gives a bank manager some indication of whether there is security for a loan.

5 Remember, tight control of cash is essential if you want to stay in business.

CASH FLOW FORECAST

Sales Receipts	1	2	3	MONTH 4	5	6	TOTAL
Total (A)	10,000	12,500	12,500	17,500	30,000	37,500	120,000
	10,000	12,500	12,500	17,500	30,000	37,500	120,000
Payments							
Raw materials	15,000	15,000	5,000	5,000	5,000	5,000	50,000
Employee wages	7,000	7,000	7,000	7,000	7,000	7,000	42,000
Overheads	6,000	6,000	6,000	6,000	6,000	6,000	36,000
Fixed Assets	10,000						
Total B	38,000	28,000	18,000	18,000	18,000		
Balances							
Cash Increase (dec.) (A)-(B)	(28,000)	(15,500)	(5,500)				
Opening balance	(10,000)	(38,000)					
Closing balance	(38,000)						

**Besides, Vivienne wants plenty of time
to teach Jack a few facts of financial life...**

The financial performance of any business is measured by a series of comparisons with other businesses, with trends over a time or with some accepted norm. These comparisons are made through calculations called **ratios.**

The ratio which so impressed your bank manager was the one which showed the amount of capital (or net assets) you employed to make your profits. This gave her a measure of your efficiency.

It's a measure of how much your business makes on the capital invested in it - a bit like the return you get on your investment in a building society. She will have looked at your net trading profit before interest on your loan or any tax was removed, and she would have made a ratio out of that figure and your net assets - both are shown on your balance sheet (p45). The resulting figure is expressed as a percentage - the higher the better. She would have taken your type of business into consideration...

It's this →

$$\text{Return on net assets} = \frac{\text{Net trading profit}}{\text{Net Assets}}$$

For instance, in the case of Giorgio, the capital employed in running this restaurant is high...

whereas Ettore, his brother, is a freelance journalist with virtually no net assets at all.

Over a year the restaurant earned £60,000 from net assets of £600,000, so its return on net assets was 10%, whereas Ettore made £30,000 using his only net asset, his computer worth £3,000 - a return of 1000%! So Ettore's return on capital appears to be much higher than Giorgio's. However, the bank would not necessarily consider him a better risk than his brother because Ettore's £30,000 was a salary as well as a return on his asset, and his investment? - 0% return on capital!

This little café bar in the middle of town is a veritable gold mine, although it might not look it. It gets crowded at lunch hours, which is more than you could say for Giorgio's! On net assets of only £50,000 it earned a mighty £25,000 last year, which is unusually high at 50%.

What's more, the proprietor pays himself £30,000 as well. So as far as the bank is concerned, the bar's a better bet.

The Return on Net Assets ratio tells you how efficient your business is

But you mustn't just wait for the figures to arrive, Jack

You have to increase profits and decrease assets to maximise this ratio. There are ways of keeping tabs on the way the business is going before it's gone, if you know what I mean.

Here's the ratio, or equation, in the box. There are other ratios which monitor the two sides of the equation, under the headings of profit managment and asset management.

$$\text{Return on net assets} = \frac{\text{Net trading profit}}{\text{Net Assets}}$$

PROFIT Management

which means monitoring

Profit margin
Contribution margin
Cost ratios

ASSET Management

which means monitoring

Asset turnover
Debtors' turnover
Stock turnover
Fixed asset turnover
Creditor turnover

First, you should maximise your profits - we call it profit management

Keep an eye on your profit margin at all times. This is the margin of profit you are making on sales - you'll want it to be as high as possible, of course.

This is the ratio for determining your profit margin

Profit margin(%) =

$$\frac{\textbf{Net profit}}{\textbf{Sales}}$$

Net profit in this case means profit before interest or tax has been deducted.

Keep your profit margin as high as possible

That's all very well, but what do you mean by 'maximise'? What if my profit margin is too low? How do I find out what's wrong?

Well, the profit margin calculation can be broken down further by reckoning something called the gross profit margin. Gross profit is the difference between sales revenue and the cost of sales - things like materials and direct labour costs to you, Jack. So if the gross profit margin is too low, either put up your prices or cut your cost of sales.

This is the ratio for determining your gross profit margin

Gross margin (%) =

$$\frac{\textbf{Gross profit}}{\textbf{Sales}}$$

Keep your gross profit margin as high as possible

The key variable costs in most businesses are materials and labour

$$\frac{\textbf{Cost of materials}}{\textbf{Sales}} \text{(\%)}$$

$$\frac{\textbf{Cost of Labour}}{\textbf{Sales}} \text{(\%)}$$

These will be very useful to you, because, while you can expect materials and labour costs to increase as your sales increase, the ratios might not change. What you will want is that they will reduce as your activity increases - and you'll want to know why not if they don't.

$$\frac{\textbf{Overhead costs}}{\textbf{Sales}} \text{(\%)}$$

You can make a similar ratio for the cost of overheads to sales, of course. There's a crucial difference here in that the overheads won't go up as the volume of sales increases, because overheads tend to be fixed.

Keep your materials, labour and overhead ratios as low as possible

Pay particular attention to those costs which are **highest and most sensitive to changes** in the market place. Whichever cost ratios you calculate, you need to find out which costs **drive** the profitability of your business

Then there's the other side of the equation - Assets

Remember the lesson the bank taught you - the bigger the profit as a proportion of its net assets, the more successful the business. So you need to keep assets low.

Return on net assets = $\dfrac{\text{Net proft}}{\text{Net assets}}$

Behind the idea of Asset Management lies the fact that profits can only be increased to a certain extent without affecting the asset base of the company, so the business's assets have to be monitored as carefully as the profits. If you were offered a £10 return on an investment, you would want to know what your outlay - your asset investment - would have to be. The basic ratio which tells you about your asset efficiency is this - *the asset turnover ratio:*

Asset turnover = $\dfrac{\text{Sales}}{\text{Net assets}}$

Don't tell me - this is another ratio I've got to keep as high as possible!

What do I do if **this** ratio isn't particularly good?

Keep an eye on it, like you did with profits. There are four areas where you can monitor your asset turnover - debtors, stock, fixed assets and creditors.

Debtors' Turnover = $\dfrac{\text{Sales}}{\text{Debtors}}$

This is an important ratio for any company selling on credit.

The debtors' turnover ratio is pretty important for your cash flow - remember Death Valley? This ratio tells you how many times debtors turnover each year. For example, in this ratio if your sales are £360,000 per annum and debtors owe £48,000 then the debtors' turnover is 7.5 p.a. (sales divided by debtors). Debtors would be paying up on average every 48.7 days (48,000 ÷ 360,000 x 365) - not bad if your credit terms are 30 days . You're right, you want to keep this ratio as high (and the average repayment time as low) as possible.

The same kind of monitoring can be done for stock, fixed assets and creditors:

Stock turnover = $\dfrac{\text{Cost of Sales}}{\text{Stock}}$	**Fixed asset turnover = $\dfrac{\text{Sales}}{\text{Fixed assets}}$**	**Creditor turnover = $\dfrac{\text{Purchases}}{\text{Creditors}}$**
Cost of sales is used because it shows the amount of stock sold.	*The smaller the amount of fixed assets that are needed to sell your goods, the better.*	*Rule of thumb: look for as much credit from your suppliers as you give to customers.*

Gearing is a term used to measure the level of borrowings of a business in relation to its resources - it's a measure of **risk**

High gearing is when the **loan capital** of a business is high. **Low gearing** when its **owner's capital** (share capital & reserves) is high. The higher the gearing, the riskier it is seen as being. The lender has less asset security against the loan, and interest payments will be less secure against fluctuations in earnings. The point is that the bank manager is as concerned about the risk she takes as she is in making a profit - after all it isn't her own money she's risking.

> Provided someone is prepared to lend it the money a business can choose the level of gearing it wishes to suit the degree of risk it is prepared to take.

Short term and long term loans

Generally, a business is better off negotiating longer term loans than short term ones. These give it security. Anyway overdrafts are repayable on demand and are therefore dangerous to count on as part of the permanent capital of the business. It's best to use overdrafts only to finance fluctuations in working capital.

The gearing ratio

A measure of the amount of external borrowing in relation to the assets of the business and is expressed by:

$$\frac{\textbf{All loans + overdraft}}{\textbf{Capital employed + overdraft}}$$

The ratio tells you how much the bank is lending compared to the shareholder's stake. Most banks think it is safe to lend up to £1 for every £1 the owners put into the business, a gearing ratio of 50%. A higher rate becomes more dangerous (80% could be fatal).

Now let me tell you a story...

It concerns two small boys, Leonard Turtis and Michael O'Hare.

No thanks

C'mon, it's easy!

PRIVATE KEEP OFF

Although they were close friends and went everywhere together it is difficult to imagine two people who were less alike. Michael was a daredevil, while Leonard was very, very cautious.

No, it's my arm, you see

Here's a nice one - power station stoker

But when they left school it was Michael who was cautious about entering into full-time employment. He spent his days at the job centre, never finding quite

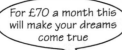

the right career for his talents. Leonard had no such trouble. He was destined for the retail trade.

Eventually Michael was taken on as a trainee salesman for a firm selling cheap computers. He needed no experience. His charm was enough.

For £70 a month this will make your dreams come true

As time went on he became sales manager, then managing director. Times were good, and the firm made huge profits by getting substantial short-term loans from the

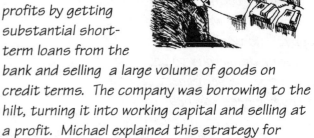

Easy!

DON'T BOTHER ME WITH DETAILS - JUST PAY!

bank and selling a large volume of goods on credit terms. The company was borrowing to the hilt, turning it into working capital and selling at a profit. Michael explained this strategy for quick profits to his friend Leonard.

Neat eh?

But aren't you trading on the bank's money? Is this legal?

Course it's legal! The bank loves it because I'm making money for them...

... and I'm paying the shareholders into the bargain. Look!

You can see that the more I borrow, the more the shareholders get. Not bad, eh?

	£ millions
Net trading profit	0.3
Interest	0.192
Profit after interest	0.108
Share capital & reserves	0.4
Return to shareholders before tax	27%

Y'see, my share capital is pretty small, but my borrowings from the bank make my capital employed up to £2 million. The shareholders are happy, because they're getting £108,000 net profit on their £400,000 stake - a 27% return

Michael's capital employed looked like this:

	£m
Share capital + reserves	0.4
Short-term loans + overdraft	1.0
Long term loans	0.6
Total	£ 2.0

The trick is, Leonard, we're borrowing at 12% and our return on capital is 15% - so the more we borrow the more we make. QED.

Michael's gearing ratio is very high...

$$\frac{£1.6m}{£2m} = 80\%$$

...and his income gearing ratio is very low...

$$\frac{\text{Net trading profit}}{\text{Interest charges}} = \frac{0.3}{0.192} = 1.56$$

...which is dangerous.

What if the return drops below the rate of interest?

It never will, my boy, it never will!

He graduated from his market barrow to a grocery shop. His growth was slow, but steady. As he expanded, he received some small loans from the bank and his first premises was mortgaged - but the loans were repaid, and his property increased in value - and after a few years he owned two shops. His family originally raised the cash to set up the business, and they are the shareholders, but they didn't see much return on their investment for a while because he reinvested every penny in his business to make it grow. His income comes from cash payments - as it always has - because he does not give credit. He is in a different position from Michael.

As time went on his activities increased in scale, so the personal touch was less in evidence. But in one important respect his business and Michael's were the same - they both made a trading profit of £300,000 in one particular pre- depression year when people were spending freely, and they both had £2 million of capital.

But what's really interesting is to compare their return to shareholders for the same period.

Michael's business was high geared whereas Leonard's had no gearing at all!

If you look at Leonard's figures you can see why:

Net trading profit (£m)	0.3	0.3
Interest	0.192	0
Profit after interest	0.108	0.3
Share capital & reserves	0.4	2.0
Return to shareholders before tax	27%	15%

Michael's return is much higher than Leonard's.

Leonard's share capital & reserves	2m
Short term loans + o'drafts	0
Long term loans	0
Net profit	0.3
Interest	0
Gearing ratio	0

Leonard had no loans!

At first sight it seemed that poor old Turtis, whose borrowing was zero, was doing less well than Michael. Turtis could pay his shareholders only 15%, while Michael could deliver a whopping 27% for the same amount of profit. He's borrowed about £1.6 million from the bank, and his shareholders are getting 3% of that because he's borrowing at 12% and making a profit on it of 15%. In good times, high gearing seems to pay!

 But then, of course, the economic climate changed and people stopped buying cheap computers, Michael's return on capital went down to 9% although he was committed to paying 12% to the bank - and his shareholders took a beating. Leonard, with his low geared company didn't notice the depression nearly as much, and continued to make a profit.

In fact, in hard times Leonard was able to pass on his economies of scale to his customers - his low gearing meant little or no interest to pay - and he wiped the floor with his competition, and got very, very rich.

Sadly, it was a different story for poor old Michael.

Enough of theory, Jack! Let's look at your accounts

Is this wise after a liquid lunch?

Come now Jack, it isn't every day that I get to lunch with an attractive, successful businessman!

Fine Furniture
Profit and loss Account
for 6 months from Jan...

	£	£
Sales		150,000
Materials	60,000	
Labour	42,000	
Factory overheads	26,000	128,000
inc dep'n & lathe rent		
Gross profit		22,000
Admin costs		12,000
Net trading profit		10,000
Interest on loan & o'draft		2,000
Net profit		8,000
Tax		2,000
Net profit after tax		£ 6,000

Here's your profit and loss forecast with the figures for your loan interest and tax in. Notice that now the bank has given you its backing you're going to have to pay for it. My estimate of that is about £2,000 in interest for the loan and overdraft over the six months, and another £2,000 for your tax bill,

Now let's make a complete balance sheet forecast and then let's analyse the lot!

Fine Furniture
Projected Balance Sheet as at 30th June ...

Where the money comes from

	£	£
Shares		15,000
Reserves		
Brought fwd	10,000	
Profit	6,000	16,000
Shareholders' funds		31,000
Loans		15,000
Capital		£ 46,000

Where the money is invested

	£	£	£
Fixed assets			17,000
Working capital			
Current assets			
Stock	14,000		
Debtors	40,000	54,000	
Current liabilities			
Creditors	(17,000)		
Overdraft	(4,000)		
Tax & interest	(4,000)	(25,000)	29,000
Net assets			£ 46,000

So, first of all we can see from the balance sheet that your return on net assets is pretty 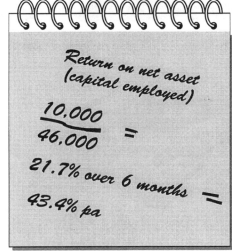 good, though not as good as the figures you gave the bank manager, because in those you hadn't made any allowance for paying tax or interest on your borrowings.

And, from the figures in the profit and loss forecast we will come up with some other ratios which are pretty reasonable too.

How do I know they are reasonable?

Return on net asset
(capital employed)

$$\frac{10,000}{46,000} =$$

21.7% over 6 months =

43.4% pa

Well, I happen to have access to figures on another company which has been around longer than you have and are a lot bigger operation - they mass-produce furniture for the trade, supplying to dealers who want high numbers of identical products.

Although they're actually making more than you are, year on year, yours is a healthier business. Just a few examples - such as return on net assets - theirs is well down on yours. They are more mechanised, but they have to pay for all that plant and their overheads are horrendous. Jaguars for all the directors - ridiculous!

I'll compare their figures to yours as I go along so you can see.

Jack's profit and cost ratios

First, Vivienne went over Jack's profit ratios (pp48 & 49)...

$$\text{Profit margin} = \frac{10,000}{150,000} = 6.7\%$$

(Chipboard's profits were £60,000 on sales of £2m, which is only 3%)

$$\text{Gross profit margin} = \frac{22,000}{150,000} = 14.7\%$$

Chipboard's material and labour costs are lower than yours because they are mechanised, and this shows itself in their higher gross profit margin - which is 20%. Their materials and labour cost ratios, which I'll show you next, are also better.

SOLD

$$\begin{array}{c}\text{Cost of materials} \\ \text{in sales}\end{array} = \frac{60,000}{150,000} = 40\%$$

(Chipboard 35%)

$$\begin{array}{c}\text{Cost of labour} \\ \text{in sales}\end{array} = \frac{42,000}{150,000} = 28\%$$

(Chipboard 22%)

$$\begin{array}{c}\text{Factory overheads} \\ \text{in sales}\end{array} = \frac{26,000}{150,000} = 17.3\%$$

(Chipboard 22%)

$$\begin{array}{c}\text{Admin costs} \\ \text{in sales}\end{array} = \frac{12,000}{150,000} = 8\%$$

(Chipboard 15%)

But their overheads and admin cost ratios are horrible - all those Jaguars! The result will be a lower profit margin for Chipboard.

The secret to success in business is efficient profit management - and efficient asset management

There's nothing to prevent you becoming as big as Chipboard - and considerably more profitable too. What your long term planning will have to focus on is the way to make your existing business more efficient without losing its character. After all, you are reasonably successful now because of the quality of furniture you produce.

But there are some things you could do without becoming another Chipboard. You might even be able to afford a Jaguar - just one, mind you!

Your ratio of overheads and admin to sales could be improved by increasing the scale of your operation. You could mechanise some of your production methods. That way you would generate more sales, so your cost ratios would go down too.

For instance, computer controlled finishing machines can prepare timber in a fraction of the time a human would take, leaving your craftsmen free to do what they do best - make high quality furniture.. You increase productivity and profit - and you don't have to turn out chipboard furniture to do it!

Intelligent use of your assets will increase the efficiency of your business.

So let's look at Asset management

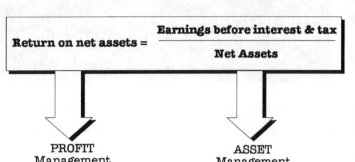

Return on net assets = $\dfrac{\text{Earnings before interest \& tax}}{\text{Net Assets}}$

↓ PROFIT
Management

which means monitoring

Profit margin
Contribution margin
Cost ratios

↓ ASSET
Management

which means monitoring

Asset turnover
Debtors' turnover
Stock turnover
Fixed asset turnover
Creditor turnover

*If we go back to the first ratio of all (p48), we've covered the left hand side - profit management. So we've only got to look at the right hand side of the equation - where we manage our assets - to see how we can become an **efficient** business.*

Remember I mentioned asset management before (p50). Let's look at how you've done.

Jack's turnover ratios

Asset turnover = $\dfrac{150,000}{46,000}$

= **3.3 times in 6 months**

which is once every 1.8 months.

Debtor turnover = $\dfrac{150,000}{40,000}$

= **3.75 times in 6 months**

which amounts to once every 1.6 months, or every 48.7 days over the 6-month period. Not very good if you're giving them only 30 days' credit!

Stock turnover = $\dfrac{128,000}{14,000}$

= **9.1 times in 6 months**

or once every 20 days. Of course, if you were to use the stock in sales for this calculation (which is more accurate) it would look better at 60,000 divided by 14,000 or 4.3 in 6 months. - or once every 42.5 days.

Creditor turnover = $\dfrac{50,000}{17,000}$

= **2.9 times in 6 months**

You repaid your creditors on average once every 63 days! Treat 'em rough, Jack!

So, after all that, how have you done?

Vivienne sums up...

Well you went to the bank thinking they were going to call in your debt and you ended up getting a long term loan. I can see why you were puzzled by that. You wouldn't have asked for more if I hadn't pushed you. The reason is that your business is fundamentally sound. Your profit margins are good because your costs are under control, and your asset management is no worse than average. So your profitability is high and that's why the bank likes you. It **wants** you to borrow money. You can make it work to their advantage

But there are two other reasons your business will succeed

1. Gearing

One is that your gearing is low. Whereas you have an overdraft and now a loan, the amount in proportion to your total business is small.

Low gearing is healthy for Jack's business, but it won't bring many smiles to his shareholders' faces. In that respect he is in Turtis's position.

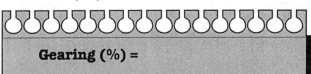

Gearing (%) =

$$\frac{\text{Long term loan + overdraft}}{\text{Capital employed + overdraft}}$$

$$= \frac{15,000 + 4,000}{46,000 + 4,000} = 38\%$$

Which is not high. The bank would have probably gone up to 50%

2. Liquidity

Liquidity depends on how full the bucket is when you need it.

Remember Death Valley? A company can be trading profitably, yet be desperately short of cash. Here's a ratio which measures the company's ability to meet its immediate liabilities...

$$\frac{\text{Current assets (cash, debtors, stock)}}{\text{Current liabilities (creditors)}} = \frac{54,000}{25,000} = 2.16$$

...out of cash, debtors and stock - all items which can be turned into cash quckly. This ratio should be as close to 1 as possible, although it will always be higher, particularly with manufacturing companies, where it could be around 2. Too many assets (e.g. too much stock) could adversely affect the return on net assets. Your current ratio is high, but safe - your debts are covered more than twice over by your current assets. But with all that money (£40,000) owing to you - unlike Turtis - you might try factoring your debtors.

So... If we take a last look at your projected balance sheet for the six months, we'll see that you will have

Maybe I can pay Auntie!

paid yourself a living wage and made £6,000 net profit. But your shareholders have a right to expect a dividend. After all, on paper they are making a return of 19.4% on their investment (that's £6,000 net profit divided by their funds of £31,000).

Maybe not.

Better than a building society by a long way. The trouble is, you have no cash. You've got an overdraft and a liquidity problem.

Fine Furniture
Projected Balance Sheet as at 30th June ...

Where the money comes from	£	£		Where the money is invested	£	£	£
Shares		15,000		Fixed assets			17,000
Reserves				Working capital			
Brought fwd	10,000			Current assets			
Profit	6,000	16,000		Stock	14,000		
				Debtors	40,000	54,000	
Shareholders' funds		31,000					
Loans		15,000		Current liabilities			
				Creditors	(17,000)		
Capital		£ 46,000		Overdraft	(4,000)		
				Tax & interest	(4,000)	(25,000)	29,000
				Net assets			£ 46,000

One solution would be to get your debtors to pay up earlier. Remember (p60) your debtors' turnover is every 48.7 days. If you could improve this by 10% - reduce your debtors from £40,000 to £36,000 - you would get rid of your overdraft! Just get the accounts settled 5 days earlier! Not too much to ask, is it? You could then think seriously about beginning to pay Auntie back.

You've done well for a first effort. I ought to take you in hand. With my brains and your cabinet making skills we'd make a wonderful team

What if it turns out to be my brains and your skills?

Meanwhile

Good evening Signor Ettore. Such a pleasure!

1 The return on net assets (or capital) ratio is the key ratio. It tells you how efficient your business is. It should be as high as possible.

2 You can improve it by managing your assets efficiently (keeping them as low as possible) and managing your profit effectively (keeping prices as high as possible and costs as low as possible).

3 Gearing measures the amount of borrowing a business has as part of its total capital. If it gets too high it can prove fatal.

4 The return to the shareholder measures how well the shareholders do from a business. If you can borrow at a rate of interest lower than the return on net assets it will be higher than the return on net assets - and vice versa.

5 The liquidity ratio measures how much cash and other liquid assets - debtors and stock - a business has compared to its current liabilities. It should be as low (close to one) as possible.

6 You compare ratios with those of other companies in the same industry, trends over time, or with some accepted norm.

Jack is showing his new finance director around the factory when...

That man looks remarkably as if he's asleep!

It's OK

That's Fergus the supervisor. He only **looks** asleep. In fact he's thinking up new products for us

Thanks for the grand tour. You know, this place could be even more profitable than Chipboard! The secret will be to keep your breakeven point low and increase your sales volume. I'll tell you what I mean in a minute. By the way, do you regard Fergus as a fixed or a variable cost?

Don't know. He's part of the production process, so... variable?

Wrong. If you have to pay him the same wage regardless of how much you produce, he's a fixed cost. I'll show you how he affects your breakeven point. In fact, I think you should know a bit more about cost, volume and prices before we go any further.

To understand your business and plan for success, you must know what your business decisions will cost. Costing is an essential ingredient of business planning.

But costing is only one part of an activity involving three elements - Prices, costs and volume, and our planning will involve all three

Each of these factors affect the other, and all of them together determine the profitablity of the company.

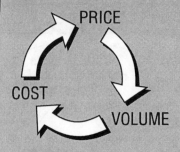

PRICE

COST

VOLUME

If you can keep your costs down you can keep your prices down and your sales volume goes up. That in turn allows you to keep your costs low by spreading your overheads over a high volume. On the other hand, if your costs are high your prices will go up and your volume down, while your overheads stay up - and the circle becomes a vicious downward spiral!

A business's decisions on prices, volume and cost are the crucial elements in planning for success.

Although the cost of something seems straightforward enough, it is not. The word "cost" is capable of many interpretations.

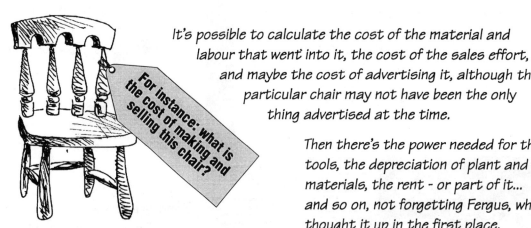

For instance: what is the cost of making and selling this chair?

It's possible to calculate the cost of the material and labour that went into it, the cost of the sales effort, and maybe the cost of advertising it, although that particular chair may not have been the only thing advertised at the time.

Then there's the power needed for the tools, the depreciation of plant and materials, the rent - or part of it... and so on, not forgetting Fergus, who thought it up in the first place.

But even if you believe you have thought of every single item which goes into making the chair, there are variables at work - what if the material costs suddenly go up in the middle of a run, or when you have to re-order? What effect does volume have on the cost of materials -are there economies of scale? Will labour costs fluctuate? In fact, what things cost in the past is called the **historic costs**. What will have more effect on your pricing will be **projected costs** - what they might be in the future.

DAILY NEWS
30% RISE IN TIMBER COSTS

Fixed costs

These are costs which do not vary with changes in the level of business activity, and they normally accrue with time. For example, if a factory is not being fully used, then no increase in the rent or rates would be necessary to increase output. These costs are fixed with respect to changes in output - up to the point when the factory is being fully utilised. In the same way, salaried staff like Fergus the supervisor would be paid the same whatever the level of output. Most overhead costs are fixed. Also, these are **committed** costs - the intention is that they will be met whatever happens. But some fixed costs are not committed: they are discretionary.

For instance, advertising is a fixed cost which can be altered at the discretion of the business, so that the decision to take a stand at a trade fair in order to attract orders would be discretionary, and, unless a contract had been signed, could be cancelled if circumstances require it.

Variable costs

These are costs which vary with the level of business activity. For example, additional expenditure would be required to provide extra materials or wages. The workers are paid on the volume they produce - like your people, Jack. In the case of factories needing to work overtime, or shops having to open over

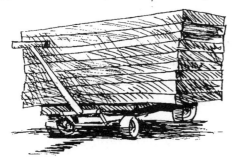

weekends the variable cost of staff is important. Some costs, like those for telephones and electricity, are partly fixed and partly variable. These are called **semi-variable,** or **semi-fixed** costs and they are only partly affected by the level of activity. The running expenses of the company van is another example of a semi-variable cost.

The breakeven point

Because the manufacture and sale of a product incurs fixed costs, some time will elapse before these costs are covered by the sales revenue. The point at which costs are met by sales is called the breakeven point. The product is not profitable until this point has been reached. Businesses offering services also have fixed setup costs which mean they will not be profitable until breakeven point is reached.

In my old company I can never remember **having** a breakeven point

It is vital to know the levels of fixed and variable costs when calculating the breakeven point

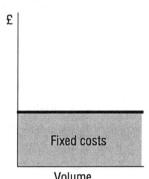

Before a business starts trading it will already have incurred fixed costs. A lease on the premises will have been signed, amenities will have been connected and staff will have started to draw their salaries. Depreciation of plant and equipment will have commenced.

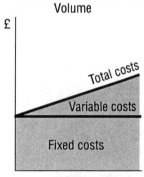

Now the business has gone into production, but none of its products or services have been sold. The variable costs are associated with the production activities of the business - the more it produces, the higher the costs.

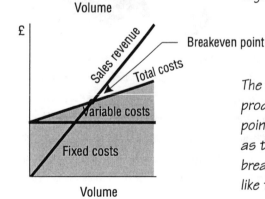

The business has now started to sell its products and is getting sales revenue. The point at which the sales revenue is the same as the total fixed and variable costs is the breakeven point. From now on, if it continues like this, the company will be profitable.

If a company breaks even at £30,000 per month, or £1,500 per working day, it is profitable if it is selling more than £1,500 worth of goods every day.

So, without having to produce any financial statements the manager knows when the business is making a profit. Trading below that figure, the manager knows the business is in trouble. The higher the breakeven point, the greater the risk of making a loss. Also, the difference between the actual sales figure and the breakeven figure can be used to work out profitability.

Champagne time, lads and lasses! Thirty three years in the business and today we've finally cracked it!

Knowing your breakeven point, you can immediately tell when you move into profit

How costs affect breakeven point

The example below shows how volume, sales revenue and costs are inter-related. The breakeven point therefore becomes an essential piece of information around which to base the plans of your business. You'll be able to estimate quickly the profit you'll make at particular activity levels, planning your business so as to maximise profits and minimise risks.

Understanding the relationship between these factors is the basis of preparing financial projections and making financial decisions..

Two companies, A and B, make the same product at the same price, but with different cost structures. A has high fixed costs but low variable costs. B has low fixed costs but high variable costs. A's breakeven point is higher than B's. At production level Z, A stands to make more profit than B, but only by taking the risk of having a higher breakeven point. If sales fall below a certain level, the siutation will change. Costs are affecting the breakeven point and therefore profit.

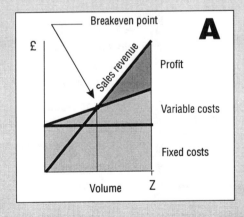

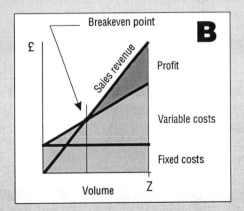

The Profit-volume chart

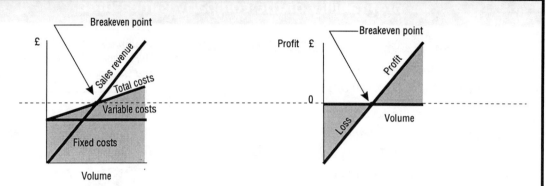

A different way of showing all this information is called the profit- volume chart (shown above on the right). It allows you to read off the profit the business will make at different levels of activity. The breakeven point is where the profit line intersects the volume axis at zero profit.

From this you can calculate how much of any particular product you have to make and sell to arrive at a given profit.
The same principle applies to services if you treat a "unit of service" (e.g. hourly consultancy rate) the same as a "unit of production".

For example:

It's £1200 before I even get in the car!

Over a year, a taxi travels 40,000 miles, charging a fare of 60p per mile. Its variable costs are 6p per mile for petrol and oil and 2p per mile for maintenance. The owner pays £140 for insurance, £100 for car tax and sets aside £960 for depreciation.
So:

		£
Revenue 40,000 x 60p		24,000
Variable costs:	£	
Petrol, oil x 6p	2,400	
Maintenance x 2p	800	
Total Variable costs	3,200	
Fixed costs:		
Insurance	140	
Car tax	100	
Depreciation	960	
Total fixed costs	1,200	
Total costs		4,400
Profit	£	19,600

Of course, the number of miles the taxi actually travels depends on how much trade it picks up. It might not be 40,000. If it is less, the owner will make less than £19,600. Below a certain mileage, he will actually lose money - after all, his fixed costs are £1,200. So what does his profit-volume line look like? Try drawing it before you look at the next page.

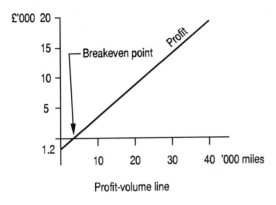

Profit-volume line

Notice you have two points which enable you to draw the line:

1 Maximum loss £1,200 - the taxi's fixed costs at zero miles.

2 £19,600 profit at 40,000 miles.

The breakeven point is 2,308 miles, or £1,385 revenue. You can calculate this, as you'll see in the following pages.

Presenting information in this way allows the taxi driver to see at a glance the profit he will make at any particular mileage.

Predicting the future

As well as analysing the present performance of the business, the diagrammatic model can be used to project "what if" situations. But in order to forecast the way the business will probably behave in the future, we need to understand the idea of *contribution...*

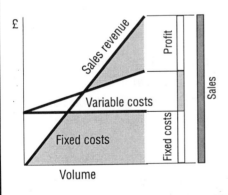

As a company goes about its business of manufacturing products or providing services, the more it sells, the more its variable costs rise and the more its sales revenue rises. The difference detween the variable costs and the sales revenue is called the **contribution** - the contribution the sales of that product or service makes to the company's fixed costs . Once all the fixed costs have been met, beyond the breakeven point all contribution is profit. Above breakeven point, another way of describing contribution is fixed costs plus profit.

Contribution = Sales - variable costs

The higher the contribution the better

This means that the taxi driver's contribution (p70) would be
sales £24,000 - variable costs £3,200 = £20,800
or,   the other way, fixed costs £1,200 + £19,600 profit = £20,800.

The contribution is the basis for two important calculations.

1. Contribution margin

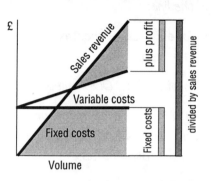

The contribution margin is very useful in forecasting the profitability of the business. If the manager can work out the contribution margin he or she can expect from the company's sales, he or she will be able to calculate the breakeven point in sales. The higher the contribution margin the better, because as you can see below, the higher it is, the lower the breakeven point.

The contribution margin is the contribution divided by total sales revenue, expressed as a percentage:

$$\text{Contribution margin} = \frac{\text{Contribution}}{\text{Sales revenue}} \quad (\%)$$

The higher the contribution margin the better

The contribution margin is the relationship between sales revenue and variable costs, and will be different for every product or service sold by a business.

A contribution margin of 60% means that of every £100 of sales, you are contributing £60 to the fixed costs of the company. Zero variable costs would mean 100% contribution towards fixed costs. Therefore the higher the contribution margin the better.

2. Breakeven point

Thie contribution margin ratio is important when calculating the breakeven point of your sales - the point at which you begin to make a profit.. The breakeven point is calculated by dividing fixed costs by contribution margin:

$$\text{Breakeven sales} = \frac{\text{Total fixed costs}}{\text{Contribution margin}}$$

The lower the breakeven sales figure the better

Remember the example of the taxi driver...

The taxi's contribution margin can be worked out as:

$$\frac{\text{Sales revenue - variable costs per mile}}{\text{Sales revenue}} = \frac{60 - 8p}{60} = 87\%$$

And the breakeven sales are the total fixed costs divided by the contribution margin

$$\text{Breakeven} = \frac{\text{Total fixed costs of £1,200}}{\text{Contribution margin of 87\%}} = £1,385$$

So the taxi owner begins to make a profit after he has taken £1,385, or travelled 2,308 miles. (The breakeven chart is on p71). What this example shows is that you should:

Keep your breakeven point as low as possible and your contribution margin as high as possible

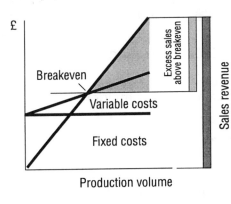

Once you know your breakeven point you have your own accounting system to calculate profit. The profit (or loss) that you are making is the gap between sales and breakeven multiplied by your contribution margin.

When you are operating above breakeven, the gap between sales and breakeven is known as the margin of safety.

A company with sales of £43,000 and a breakeven of £33,000 at a contribution margin of 40% would have figures like this

Sales	£43,000
Breakeven	£33,000
	£10,000
Profit @ 40%	£4,000

$$\text{Margin of safety is} \quad \frac{10,000}{43,000} = 23.3\%$$

If the same company had a turnover of only £23,000 it would be operating below breakeven and making a loss of £10,000 x 40% = £4,000.

Obviously, there is no margin of safety.

$$\text{Margin of safety} = \frac{\text{Excess sales above breakeven}}{\text{Sales revenue}}$$

The higher the margin of safety the better.

What all these calculations enable you to do, Jack, is get a clear idea of what your business is like; how it's doing, what its profitability will be under certain circumstances, and what it will be if they change. It gives you control. Even when everybody has gone home it's possible to see exactly how you are doing. At the beginning, you were looking all around the place trying to find that out. Now you can know, by understanding how business finance works.

For instance, having worked out the contribution margin and breakeven point, you can calculate your profit or loss quickly, based upon your sales, without waiting for a profit and loss statement. Here's an example, using what I think our own figures could be:

If I know that my breakeven point is, say, £30,000 per month, then at £50,000 sales I am £20,000 above breakeven.

Suppose my contribution margin is 25% - not very high, incidentally, then my clear pre-tax profit will be £20,000 x 25%, or £5,000.

This gives me my margin of safety. Remember:

$$\text{Margin of safety} = \frac{\text{Sales above breakeven}}{\text{Actual sales}} \text{ as a percentage}$$

So, in this example the safety margin would be $\frac{20,000}{50,000}$ or **40%**

If these figures are right, we're in pretty good shape.

The higher the safety margin, the lower the risk to the business

Making decisions

But the real power of having the company's figures at your finger-tips is in your ability to make financial decisions which can increase your future profitability - or at least avoid disaster.

Gentlemen, I am empowered on the basis of last year's figures to make my recommendation to the Board, and it is...

RUN FOR YOUR LIVES!

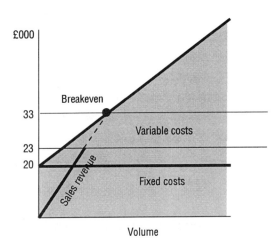

Suppose you have, as in the example on page 73, a breakeven point of £33,000 per month, with a contribution margin of 40%, and you are making a *loss* of £10,000 - i.e. you have a turnover of £23,000. What can you do?

Here are two alternatives, with their consequences:

1 Increase sales

← This where you are when you start. You decide to advertise. Your advertising budget is £14,000.

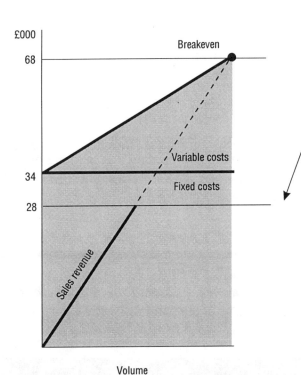

Result

Your sales have gone up from £23,000 to £28,000 but your advertising has pushed your fixed costs up. The additional £14,000 on your fixed costs means that your breakeven point has gone up by £14,000 ÷ 40% = £35,000. Instead of breaking even at sales of £33,000 you would now need sales of £68,000. So to breakeven you have to more than double sales! It's unlikely this would work.

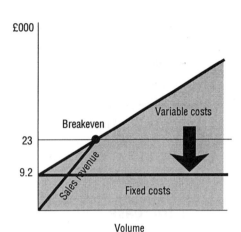

2 Force down the breakeven

You can do this by forcing down your fixed costs, i.e. by becoming more efficient. Look at that advertising budget again. Economise on office costs. Sublet some unused buildings etc. Your fixed costs would have to come down to £9,200 to breakeven at sales of £23,000 (£23,000 x 40%).

Or

You can reduce your variable costs, thus increasing your contribution margin. If you did this your contribution margin would have to go up to 87% (£20,000 ÷ £23,000).

Another way to raise your contribution margin would be to raise your price, if you believe the market would bear it. Selling less at a higher price will reduce your volume, but it will also improve your contribution margin and so lower your breakeven point. You might therefore end up making higher profit. But beware the downward spiral (p66).

The key to control is an understanding of breakeven and contribution. It enables you to monitor your business's performance day by day and to be flexible.

Minimise your breakeven point. Maximise your margin of safety

Sub-contracting

Another six months have passed. Fine Furniture is now a well-run and successful company. All its workshop staff are on regular weekly wages, and the order book is healthy, although not completely full...

when...

Hey Viv, you want to hear the good news?

Or the bad news?

Name's Vivienne, stranger, and gimme the good news first

An order for 1000 school desks at £60 every year for 3 years!

And don't tell me - the bad news is we need extra plant to do the job

I know we've got some spare capacity, Jack, but we'd need an extra routing machine and finisher, and our fixed costs are still too high. Let's look into sub-contracting.

Bear with me, Jack. Just listen to Mr Joiner's proposal. We don't have to take it

We are bound to be able to do it cheaper. Common sense

RELIABLE JOINERS LTD

My best price is £30 each, delivered

Listen, we can make them for £22 each

Ssh! One word - depreciation

We are going to have to buy £40,000 worth of equipment to do this job. Straight line depreciation over 5 years means that we'd have to make £8,000 in order to cover the depreciation costs of the equipment - and bear in mind that the school contract is only for 3 years.

£40,000

Buy-in price per 1000 desks	£ 30,000

Costs of our production

Materials	9,000
Variable overheads	13,000
Machinery deprec'n	8,000
Our total costs	£ 30,000

Sure it would only cost us £22 each for labour, materials and the other direct overheads, but depreciation in this case would mean that we would have to find work for our new machinery for another two years to break even on this deal. No, let Reliable Joiners do the depreciating!

Keep your fixed costs as low as possible. Maximise your contribution margin and keep your breakeven point low

Vivienne has asked Jack and Andy into her office. She is going to give them the latest sixth-monthly results.

Because you've been keeping a careful eye on costs, and because we subcontracted where necessary, we've done quite well in the last six months. In fact, we've paid off our short term loan - and you'll be pleased to hear we're in a position to give Auntie something at last. Here are the results...

Fine Furniture
Profit and loss Account
for the year from Jan...

	£	£
Sales		300,000
Materials	105,000	
Labour	75,000	
Factory overheads	50,000	230,000
inc dep'n & lathe rent		
Gross profit		70,000
Admin costs		-30,000
Net trading profit		40,000
Interest on loan & o'draft		-4,000
Net profit		36,000
Tax		-10,000
Net profit after tax		£ 26,000

Our admin costs are up because of my salary; but our cost ratios are better - I'll leave you gentlemen to work them out for yourselves! From what I've told you, work out the costs of materials, labour, factory overheads and gross and net profit margins. And while you're at it, calculate the stock, debtor, creditor and assets turnovers; and tell me what our return on capital and return to shareholders is.* You may be pleasantly surprised!

Answers on page 90.

Fine Furniture
Balance Sheet
as at 31 December ...

	£	£	£
Fixed assets			17,000
Working capital			
Current assets			
Stock	23,000		
Cash	6,000		
Debtors	50,000	79,000	
Current liabilities			
Creditors		(30,000)	49,000
Net assets			66,000
Loans			(15,000)
			£ 51,000
Represented by:			
Shares			15,000
Reserves			
Brought fwd		10,000	
Profit		26,000	36,000
			£ 51,000

To do all of that, you will need our balance sheet. So I've drawn it up in line with the format required by the Companies Act. You'll notice it is a little different.

GROAN

You mean that, after all this time struggling to do it one way I've got to start all over...

No, as long as you understand that it's just a different way of presenting the same information. We normally draw it up like this...

Fine Furniture
Balance Sheet as at 31 December...

Where the money comes from	£	£		Where the money is invested	£	£	£
Shares		15,000		Fixed assets			17,000
Reserves				Working capital			
Brought fwd	10,000			Current assets			
Profit	26,000	36,000		Stock	23,000		
				Cash	6,000		
Shareholders' funds		51,000		Debtors	50,000	79,000	
Loans		15,000					
				Current liabilities			
Capital		£ 66,000		Creditors		(30,000)	49,000
				Net assets			£ 66,000

Fine Furniture Balance Sheet as at 31 December ...	£	£	£
Fixed assets			17,000
Working capital			
Current assets			
Stock	23,000		
Cash	6,000		
Debtors	50,000	79,000	
Current liabilities			
Creditors		(30,000)	49,000
Net assets			66,000
Loans			(15,000)
			£ 51,000
Represented by:			
Shares			15,000
Reserves			
Brought fwd		10,000	
Profit		26,000	36,000
			£ 51,000

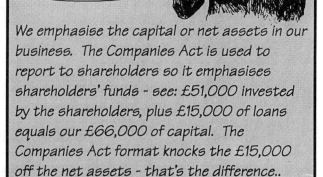

Notice that the Companies Act uses what's called a 'vertical format' while we use a 'horizontal format'

We emphasise the capital or net assets in our business. The Companies Act is used to report to shareholders so it emphasises shareholders' funds - see: £51,000 invested by the shareholders, plus £15,000 of loans equals our £66,000 of capital. The Companies Act format knocks the £15,000 off the net assets - that's the difference..

Work out our performance for yourself. Then, I think we both need a holiday!

With no short term debts and cash of £6,000, Auntie's dividend is going to be quite good. She invested £10,000, which is 2/3 of the total shares, so she gets 2/3 of the cash dividend, or £4,000. Even though she has had to wait quite a long time to get it, it's better than the return from a building society, and it should get better year by year from now on.

6 Summary

1 The breakeven point is the benchmark against which the profitability of the company can be measured. Keep it as low as possible to minimise your risk.

2 Breakeven point is calculated as

$$\frac{\text{Total fixed costs}}{\text{Contribution margin}}$$

3 The margin of safety is a measure of the riskiness of the business. Keep it as high as possible.

4 Margin of safety is calculated as

$$\frac{\text{Excess above breakeven}}{\text{Sales revenue}}$$

5 You need to know your contribution margin to make financial decision - whether to incur the additional fixed costs of an advertising campaign (how much more sales are needed), whether to subcontract production and the likely effect of increasing your prices.

Well, Viv, I'm looking forward to a couple of weeks without accounts

Yes, here's to a rest in the Dodecanese!

Meet my favourite island

What a lovely, restful life this must be, Jack

Petros, old friend, meet my, er, Finance Director, Viv

To you, Viv this is paradise. To us...

Do call me Vivienne

...to us, living is hard. We must make what we can of tourism in the summer now that the fishing is getting more difficult. May I say, you are our main source of income.
For myself, I have a dilemma concerning my little business. How would you advise?

I own the Kyristanis, a boat which is capable of holding 25 passengers. With myself, the crew consists of Lefkis and Yanni. We must make much of the summer to sustain us in the winter, when there is no work. We take our guests on two - day trips

around the islands. The crew arrange barbecue feasts and tented accommodation for one night.

"We also include a free evening meal in a taverna, and a picnic and swim. For this we ask 20,000 drachma from each guest. I believe this to be fair. However, sometimes I can get barely ten tourists to embark on our pleasure trip. So what I would beg of you, fair Finance Director, is at what point do I cancel the trip? At ten? At fourteen? I should be grateful were you to enlighten me."

OK Petros, tell me the answers to these questions...

How much does the boat cost to run?
How often are your trips?
Is the trip always the same - same taverna, same picnics, same length?
What does the fuel cost?
How much a head do you pay the taverna?

Let's see, with depreciation, dock dues, crew, maintenance...160,000 drachmas a week. One trip every week. Everything is exactly the same. Sometimes the weather is a little rough, but....
Fuel always about 80,000 drachmas.
4,000 for the taverna, all food drink and picnic provisions.

The figures you've given me are these:

Fixed cost (drachmas)	160,000
Variable cost per passenger	4,000
cost per ticket	20,000
Fuel bill	80,000
Boat holds 25 maximum	

Well, your fixed costs are 160,000, to which you can add your fuel bill because it's always 80,000, totalling 240,000. As far as variable costs go, each tourist pays 20,000, but it costs you 4,000, so their contribution is 16,000 (or contribution margin 80% of the sales revenue which is pretty good). Our formula for breakeven point is total fixed costs divided by contribution margin, which is 240,000 / 80%.

So you have to take 300,000 drachmas - or 15 tourists - to break even. Every tourist over that figure is profit!

That means a maximum profit of 10 x 16,000, or 160,000 drachmas per trip.

Amazing! In one way I now regret the inadequacy of my philosophy degree. One more small problem and then you are my guests for dinner

The problem concerns my family, who own Peros Beach. We need to replace the bed-chairs which have been there , well, too long. Our dilemma is whether to buy cheaper beds at 10,000 drachmas each or more expensive ones at 13,333. We need 15 beds - the beach will take no more - and we are competing with the other beach, which has good beds. I have said go for the better beds and charge a little extra at 3600 drachmas, but my brothers want to buy the cheaper ones and stay at the present rate of 3500. I know I am right, because my bed chairs will need less attention. The canopies automatically fold when not in use, whereas the others need an extra hour to be put away. I can negotiate 1100 drachmas a day with the attendant for the better bed chairs, against the 1500 we are paying for cheap beds already. What is your view?

To be home an hour earlier is a blessing!

OK, you've got the choice of 2 beds, bed A and bed B, right? Bed A works out at 150,000 for the 15, bed B at 200,000, or each of A at 10,000 and each of B at 13,333. Now let's work out your breakeven point.

	Bed A	Bed B
Hire cost per bed day	3500	3600
Variable cost per bed day	1500	1100
Contribution	2000	2500
Contribution margin	57%	69%
Breakeven point	approx 262,500	approx 288,000

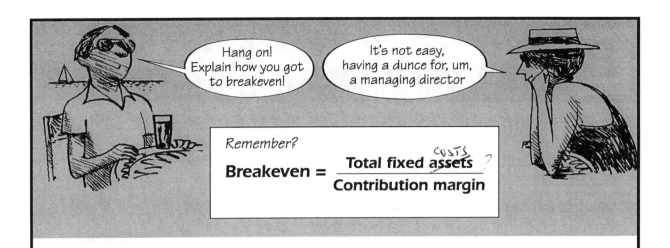

So in the case of bed A the breakeven is 150,000 / 57%, which is around 262,500 dracks, and in the case of bed B is 200,000 / 69%, or approximately 288,000 dracks. Or, to put it into terms the attendant could understand, you'd have to hire out each of beds A 75 times or each of beds B 80 times to break even. It's up to Petros to decide whether people will like the better beds enough to enable him to reach his higher target. This is a marketing decision. I'm only a finance director.

Asset	The property of the company, such as land, buildings, stocks etc.
Asset turnover	A measure of how effectively assets are used. It should be as high as possible.
Balance sheet	A snapshot picture of the assets and liabilities of a business. It tells you where the money in a business came from and into what assets it has been invested.
Breakeven point	The point at which sales equal total costs and no profit is made. Sales above this point generate profit. Sales below this point lead to losses.
Capital	Normally means permanent or long-term funds of the business: shareholders' funds and long-term loans. Often misused, so safest to ask for a definition.
Cash	What you normally buy things with. Without it you go bankrupt. Cash in a balance sheet may be in the bank or in petty cash.
Cash flow	Normally this means the amount of cash coming in and going out of a business in a particular period.
Contribution	The difference between sales revenue and variable costs.
Creditors	The money the business owes to another for goods and services provided but not paid for.
Current asset	Assets held by a business for a short period (under 12 months) in the course of trading (stock, debtors, cash).
Current liability	Debt or liability due within 12 months (e.g. creditors, overdraft).
Debt	Money owed to other people such as loan capital, creditors or bank overdraft.

Debtors	The money owed to the business by customers who have received goods or services but not yet paid for them.
Debtor turnover	A measure of how quickly debtors pay up. It can be expressed in days or in the number of times debtors 'turnover' or pay up each year.
Depreciation	A charge against profit to represent the wearing out of a fixed asset. A proportion of the cost of the asset is charged to the profit of each period over the asset's life.
Dividend	Amounts paid by a company to shareholders out of profits as a return to the shareholder. There is no automatic entitlement to a dividend.
Equity	Same as shareholders' funds.
Factoring	A form of finance whereby cash is provided against your sales invoices, normally 80% of the invoice value. A charge of 2.5 - 4% above base rate is made for this.
Fixed assets	Long-term assets of a business used in the production of goods and services: land, buildings, vehicles, office equipment, computers, plant and machinery. Things you do not intend to resell in the course of trade.
Fixed costs	Costs that do not vary with changes in trading activity volume.
Gearing	A measure of borrowed money against shareholders' funds. Often used very loosely.
Gross profit	Difference between sales revenue and the cost of making whatever was sold.

Income statement	Same as profit and loss account.
Indirect costs	Same as overheads.
Liability	Amounts owed to others by the company.
Loan capital	Long-term loans (due over one year hence).
Loss	An excess of expenses over sales revenues.
Margin of Safety	The extent above breakeven that the company is operating at. It tells you about the riskiness of the business, and should be as high as possible.
Net assets	Fixed assets plus current assets less current liabilities.
Net current assets	Same as working capital.
Net trading profit	Gross profit minus overhead costs.
Overdraft	A credit facility arranged with a bank which is variable in amount but which must be repaid on demand. Interest is charged on the balance outstanding on a daily basis.
Overheads	Expenses that cannot easily be attributed or traced to particular products or processes.
Prepayment	An advance payment by your company. A current asset.
Profit	An increase in the net assets of a business brought about by trading such that sales revenue exceed expenses. Not to be confused with cash flow.
Profit and loss account	Detailed information on sales, expenditure and hence profit or loss in a trading period. However, the terms can also mean the same as 'reserves'.
Profit and loss statement	Same as profit and loss account but only for a trading period.

Loss

Profit

Reserves or retained earnings or retained profit	Accumulated and undistributed profits from previous periods.
Return on capital or return on net assets	A measure of how effectively the company is trading.
Return on shareholders' funds	A measure of the return the shareholders are getting from their investment in the company (from trading and using loan capital).
Share capital	Capital put into the business by the shareholders or owners. If the company fails, the shareholder can lose this money.
Shareholders' funds	Share capital plus reserves and profit or loss for the period.
Stock	Those assets which are resold by the business in the course of trade. Stock can be raw materials, work-in-progress or finished goods. In the USA, stock refers to share capital.
Stock turnover	A measure of how quickly stock is used. It can be expressed in days or in the number of times stock is used each year.
Total assets	Fixed assets plus current assets.
Turnover	The same as sales.
Undistributed profit	Same as reserves.
Variable costs	Costs that vary with changes in the level of activity of the business (e.g. materials costs).
Working capital	Current assets less current liabilities. This is the capital that is working for the company and is constantly turning over.

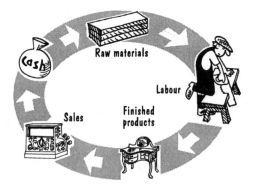

Answer page

The final accounts of Fine Furniture on page 80 gave all the figures necessary to make the calculations showing the financial health of the company. If you want to try your hand (don't cheat, the answers are upside down at the bottom of this page) we give you the page numbers where you'll find the necessary ratios. The important thing to bear in mind, more than arriving at the right figures, is that you should understand the need for them.

Work out, using the profit and loss account:

- a.   Cost of materials in sales (p49)
- b.   Cost of labour in sales (p49)
- c.   Cost of factory overheads in sales (p49)
- d.   Gross profit margin (p49)
- e.   Admin cost in sales (overhead costs p49)

And use the figures in the balance sheet to work these out:

- f.   Stock turnover (p50)
- g.   Debtor turnover (p50)
- h.   Creditor turnover (p50)
- i.   Asset turnover (p50)
- j.   Gearing (p51)
- k.   Liquidity (p61)

What is the return on capital (net assets) for the final figures? (p48). Answer l. And what will Auntie get after tax and interest? (Compare the net profit to the shareholders' funds). Answer m.

How do these results compare with the previous set of figures (Jack's forecasts on pp44 and 45)?

Push the boat out, Auntie!

I knew I could count on you, Jack dear!

a. 35% b. 25% c. 16.6% d. 23.3% e. 10% f. x10 g. x6 h. x3.3 i. x4.5
j. 22.7% which is low because only the long term loan is left k. 2.6 (very safe)
l. 60.6% for the year - pretty good
m. 51% for the year after tax (70.5% before tax) - very good!